Endless Possi

My Fresh S

By

Matthew Ingram

Rob,

Hope you enjoy reading

my story.

All the best,

Smiler

Dedication

In memory of Richard Kelley

Disclaimer

This book is a memoir. It reflects the author's present recollections of experiences over time. Some names and characteristics have been changed, some events have been compressed, and some dialogue has been recreated.

Foreword

I lie on a grubby sofa, staring at the flickering light of an electric fire, swallowing my third, or maybe fourth, tab of LSD in half an hour. The LSD is a last-ditch attempt to keep the party going. It's not my drug of choice, but I've run out of cocaine and alcohol, and sobriety isn't an option. Neither is sleep, because sleep means sobering up, and I can't face the thought of that.

This isn't my flat. It's my friend Gavin's. I've left my parents' house again, tired of them nagging at me, tired of seeing the worry in their eyes. It's easier just to avoid it, and so I've run away. Around me lie bags and bags of dirty clothes. I can't be bothered to do any laundry, so I just buy more clothes. I have the money, after all; there are thousands still left in my bank account from an inheritance payment a few months ago. Gavin has gone to bed. He's sick of me now. Everyone is. Nobody knows what to do with me.

I've been up for days on end at this point. Four? Or is it five? I can't remember. I've been carried away on a drink and drugs binge that has blurred all my sense of time. I'm doing fine though. I know this because I'm staying away from crack cocaine. Yes, I'm doing anything else I can get my hands on to keep my mind off it, but that doesn't count. Crack is my problem, and I'm off that. I'm fine.

Suddenly, there are people in the flat. Crowds and crowds of people, shouting at me, chasing me, with evil in their eyes, and weapons in their hands. I know they are not real, but they feel very real, and I am utterly terrified. I leap up, gathering together a pile of Gavin's shoes. In a panic, I begin throwing them at my attackers, screaming at them to go away.

They do. They just vanish. Disaster averted. I stagger back to the sofa, and stare at the fire again. I am still exhausted, yet I am still desperately fighting sleep.

As I look at the flames, they begin to grow, dancing across the carpet, and creeping further into the room. I sit up once more. I am in a top floor flat, and it's on fire. I can hear voices from inside the flames, screaming in terror. *Help us*, they say, *save our children*.

I run to the window in a panic and look down. I can hear more voices now. *Jump*, they say, *jump now*. I don't jump. I can't bring myself to. But I feel as though I am losing my mind with fear. Somehow, I end up back on the sofa, my head echoing with the voices of the people coming from the flames.

I wake up later that evening, sweating and pale, with a rancid taste in my mouth. The light is fading, and I feel utterly miserable. This is the worst comedown I have ever had. I begin to gather my many shopping bags together. I know it's time for me to leave Gavin's now.

Out of options, I crawl back to my parents, out of drugs and booze, and shaking with fatigue. They are not speaking to me – this is normal by now. I sit on the sofa and I think how badly I want to die. This is the most actively suicidal I have ever felt, and I feel myself making plans. I know that I am going to get in my car, and I am going to drive really fast into a bridge. I'm going to take my seatbelt off right before I hit the wall, just to make sure. I'm going to do this very soon.

Right now, though, I am too tired to do anything. I crawl to bed and sleep for 48 hours, my body aching with tiredness. It's a deep sleep, dark and all-consuming. It's the sleep of someone who has truly run themselves into the ground.

Two days later, I wake up. I feel better. I am no longer suicidal. It must just have been a bad day. And so, of course, I start again. What else is there to do? I don't have a job. I don't have commitments. The only thing in my life is drugs, and I cannot see it any other way. *I'm normal*, I tell myself, *I'm fine*. I pull my shoes on and head straight out to the pub.

And the miserable cycle begins again.

Chapter One

My early life held no warning signs of what was to come. If you had told my parents that I would grow up trailing chaos in my wake in the way I did, they would have been completely shocked. I didn't fit in with the typical image of a Class A drug user, and I still don't. What I've learned through my experiences and my journey from addiction into sobriety, is that there truly is no 'typical' user. Addiction is a horrible disorder that can absolutely take hold of anyone, and our life experiences prior to that only form part of the picture.

This is the winding tale of the path that led me to drug addiction. It's not an excuse, or a way of pinning the blame on anyone else. I'm not trying to justify my choices, or the decisions I made. What I am hoping to do is to provide an explanation, and an illustration of the series of events and life choices that pulled me down that road. This is my story.

***

I am the second of two children; my older brother, David, arrived four years before I did. Despite a miscarriage the year before I was born, my mum was much more relaxed in her pregnancy with me. In a true display of the times, she smoked the whole way through, cutting down, but never stopping entirely. She was also unpleasantly ill through most of the pregnancy, with vomiting and heartburn.

'You were such a pain towards the end', she used to tell me, and I will admit it sounds unpleasant; I was 10 days overdue, and Mum spent much of that time perched upright on the sofa, unable to sleep or even move without discomfort. By the time I finally made my appearance she was more than ready for me.

My birth was, as all births are, dramatic in its own way. The day was gloomy, the air hanging heavy with the threat of rain, and Mum's pains were so frequent she turned up with my dad at St Paul's Maternity Hospital demanding to be admitted.

'It's not time,' the admissions nurse told her, barely holding back an eye roll. Nurses at maternity units are used to panicking

1

women in the early stages of labour. Mum, however, was having none of it. She was being admitted, and wasn't going home.

'It is definitely time,' snapped Mum, 'this is exactly what happened with my first. I'm not going anywhere.'

The nurse glanced around and sighed reluctantly. The labour ward was quiet, and Mum was quite clearly digging her heels in.

'Fine, you can stay and be monitored. But I'm telling you, your waters haven't broken – it's going to be a while yet.'

Not half an hour later Mum was in full labour, teeth gritted, no pain relief except gas and air, screaming about how she didn't have the rocking chair she requested, and no, she didn't want the music she'd brought.

I came into the world at 7:15pm. In another strange sign of the times, my dad went home after Mum was admitted to the postnatal ward. As soon as she could, she nipped outside for a Twix and a cigarette, coming back to find me happy and contented. We went home together the next day.

And so began my life.

I was a happy baby, always laughing, and relentlessly cheerful. I very rarely cried or threw fits. Even a hernia operation at three months old didn't faze me; my mum remembers me being wheeled back from surgery laughing in the middle of my wide hospital bed.

My early childhood paints a similar picture of sweetness and light. I was a joy to be around, curious, funny and kind. I was easy to please, never asking for anything, even when in the magical land that was Toys R Us. One Christmas, when I was around five years old, I got just one small gift, while Dave opened what seemed like an endless pile of presents in front of me. It didn't bother me. I stood up, wrapped my arms around my mum, and thanked her for the best Christmas ever, at which point they revealed the bike they had hidden behind the living room curtain. My joy was indescribable.

I always felt loved and supported as a child, confident in the knowledge that my parents cared deeply for me. Mum used to tuck me into bed every single night when I was little, pulling the covers up to my chin and making sure I was comfortable and settled. Once my eyes were closed, she'd creep out of the room and down the stairs. If I was still awake and heard her leaving, I'd sit up in bed and shout out 'I love you' every time she went down a step. She would shout it back. Our home was always filled with love.

My parents loved each other very much as well. Mum and Dad were (and still are) extremely happy together, and he continues to pride himself on how well he looks after her. Each morning he makes her coffee while she's in the shower and straightens up the bed, a tradition that's been going on for as long as I can remember. They are very firmly nestled in their happy routine, and I remember nothing but harmony as I was growing up.

When I was a young child, my dad did night shifts at a switchboard and Mum worked during the day. In the early evenings they would swap over the childcare, but never before having a cup of tea together, and carefully dissecting the time they had spent apart. They would sit at the kitchen table, Dad in his crisp white shirt and smelling of aftershave, Mum drooping from work, clutching the small amount of time they had together with both hands.

'If you've upset your mum, you've upset me,' Dad would say to me if I ever did anything wrong. I carried this through to adulthood as well, and it's something I'm still very aware of. Mum and Dad were, and are, and always have been, a team.

Sunday dinners were family time, and we would all eat together: me, Dave, Mum, Dad and Uncle Trevor. Trevor was not actually an Uncle, he was my brother's Godfather, and a friend from around the time that Mum and Dad had met at work. He was an odd character; grumpy, moody and unfathomably rude. I'm fairly sure that my parents' affection for him was at least partially borne from a sense of responsibility; it was quite clear that he had no-one else who particularly cared about him. My parents are kind and generous like that, and as a result, every Sunday he'd be there, perched on one of our chairs, glowering into the distance, failing to make any sort of conversation.

'Any roasties Trevor?' my mum would say, stood over the dinner she and Dad had slaved over for hours that morning.

3

'Here', Trevor would say, pointing at his plate, often not even making eye contact. Not only was he difficult, he also had some problematically old-fashioned views. He strongly believed that a woman's place was in the kitchen, and my mum often found herself biting her tongue around him. She must have badly wanted to snap back at him, but she always kept quiet, reminding herself that Trevor was someone to feel sorry for. He struggled hugely with his mental health, having battled with Bipolar Disorder for his entire life, and was usually heavily medicated. He was, however, hospitalized semi-regularly, usually because he'd come off his medication unsupervised. During these periods, my dad would go and visit him in hospital, and eventually he'd be stabilised, and then discharged. He'd then turn up again at Sunday dinners, mood flat, and a picture of sullen rudeness at the table. It seems odd looking back, but Trevor was a permanent fixture throughout my childhood. He later played a huge role in my adult life as well – but we'll get to that.

I started school in September 1996, when I was four years old. I went to Swindon Village Primary School, which was walking distance from where I grew up in Wymans Brook. It was a tiny school, close-knit and comfortable, and I was settled and happy. I had plenty of friends, and I very much enjoyed my time there. It felt safe and enjoyable. I loved school.

***

All of this paints a picture of a very happy childhood. And I want to make that very clear – I did have a happy childhood. I was loved and cared for, educated and well-fed. I had friends, and a supportive, kind and interested family. But despite all this, inside me there were hints of confusion and turmoil. There has always been an anxiety within me; a feeling of unease that I have carried with me for as long as I can remember.

At school I craved attention and was desperate to be fussed over. This seems at odds with the joyous picture painted above, but it wasn't – I just wanted to be cared for. I remember being intensely jealous of anyone who got injured or hurt in any way, and once I actually scraped my face on purpose, specifically so I could get some attention and care. I approached a Dinner Lady with blood beading on the graze, my eyes full of tears. The injury was surface level and barely visible, but I still got the special wet paper towel treatment, and a note written home to tell my parents about my accident. The feeling of being fussed over warmed me inside and I felt special for that short moment.

When it came to moving from primary school to secondary school, I had a choice: Cleeve, which was a better school, and where most of my friends were going; or Pittville, which was closer. I chose Pittville simply because I didn't want to take the bus. Or that was the excuse I used to explain it to my mum anyway; in truth, the entire concept of Cleeve made me anxious. I was used to closeness and smallness, and the soft comfort blanket of being in a tiny school close to home had in no way prepared me for the big wide world. Everything about moving up and changing school seemed utterly overwhelming, and so I dug my heels in and went for the safer option.

It wasn't just the outside world that worried me. Home also caused my anxiety to spike at times. David and I had an intense sibling rivalry that could often turn into powerful squabbles that got very physical.

'Fatso!' I would shriek at him, the final blow in an argument that usually began with the remote control, or something equally trivial. This would cause him to erupt, and he'd charge towards me in rage, threatening to sit on me, and regularly following through with that. He was much bigger than me, and when he attacked me physically it genuinely scared me. I quickly learned to lock myself in the bathroom whenever he came running towards me, and I have vivid memories of hammering up the stairs, propelled by complete terror.

Once, Dave hovered threateningly on the landing when I locked myself in. He was clearly waiting for me to make my escape, and I was shaking with fear, perched on the side of the tub. I was listening as carefully as I could for any signs of movement, so I could flee to safety.

Nothing.

I placed my ear to the door, and heard only silence. He had definitely gone. I carefully eased open the bathroom door and put my foot through the doorway, preparing to run.

Suddenly, he appeared, launching out of nowhere and slamming the door directly onto my foot. The pain was explosive and I screamed out and stumbled backwards. He leapt on top of me on the tiled floor and began to lay into me, landing blows on my face and stomach. The pain of that was nothing compared to my foot, and I submitted in tears.

These fights were absolutely the product of both of us; I was in no way continuously terrorized by Dave, and I absolutely played my part in the fights and the screaming matches. I do, however, remember how scared I became when he ran at me, and the pit of fear in my stomach whenever we fought. There was little support from my parents over mine and Dave's fights – or at least that's the way I remember it. They were seen as amusing squabbles, and both Mum and Dad adopted a 'boys will be boys' attitude towards the rough and tumble. They refused to split us up, or to ever take sides.

Family life generally caused me a huge amount of anxiety. Dinner times were full of rules: food to mouth, not mouth to food; elbows off the table; finish your food and your water before you're allowed to leave the table. If we broke these rules the response would be explosive; shouting and sometimes silent treatment.

I often felt like I was walking on eggshells round my own house; a knot of worry would form in my stomach, and I'd feel stressed and uncomfortable. My memory is that I was always the one being shouted at or told off; that no-one else in the house could put a foot wrong. I don't know how true this is really; memory is very subjective, but what is undeniable is the fact that I felt different, and at times very isolated.

Many addicts report this feeling of being different, and this was a thread that ran through my life. I felt that I was unusual in some way, like my way of thinking left me on a different level to other people. I was constantly concerned about doing something wrong, or about not being liked by the people around me. It was an uncomfortable feeling, and often very lonely. I did my best to avoid it when I could.

The worry I felt bled into my social life and how I acted at school. I hid my anxiety and discomfort behind a mask that I discovered early and then wore for years; that of the class clown. This was a technique that worked well for me; I became popular, funny and well-liked in school, and thus immune to any bullying or disrespect. Playing the Joker in class also gave me a role and a purpose, and allowed me to become someone else for a while.

My impersonations of the teachers at school always went down well, and quickly became legendary. One particular teacher, Mr. Sullivan, had a good sense of humour himself, and asked me to impersonate him for everyone. He was a caricature of a man; American and short in stature. I burst in through the classroom door screaming in his thick Buffalo accent, shuffling on my knees, and the room erupted in explosive laughter. It was one of my finer moments and the glow of pleasure it gave me was unparalleled.

My behaviour in school often got me into trouble, although this was a price that I considered more than worth paying for the attention and validation I got. I was regularly given detentions, both at lunchtime and after school, which my parents were notified about by a letter to the house. I prided myself on my ability to intercept and destroy these letters, and for years my parents remained convinced that I was a diligent student who did a wide range of after school activities. My luck finally ran out after I was excluded for hitting someone who was picking on someone else. My mum went to see the headmaster in my defence.

'It's very unlike Matt to do anything wrong!' exclaimed Mum, amused by the thought that her son could have behaved badly.

'Oh really?' said the head, also amused, but for an entirely different reason. She pulled out my healthy-sized record of detentions and punishments and slid it across the table.

'Oh,' said Mum, leafing through it. She looked up at me, concerned, but I waved it off.

'I'm doing fine, Mum,' I said, and she nodded. She had no reason not to believe me, and I believed it myself. I was in control.

I oozed confidence when I was Matt the Clown, in a way that I didn't when I was just myself. The laughter of others became my fuel. I was at my happiest when people were laughing with me, and it rapidly became a coping mechanism that I carried forward throughout my adult life. Even now I find myself switching to humour in uncomfortable situations, a natural reaction whenever anything becomes uncomfortable.

***

My rebellious behaviour extended outside of class as well, and I soon began smoking. The first time I tried a cigarette was with two girls from school, whose names are far less important than the cigarette in this story. I was around 11 or 12, impressionable and obsessed with cultivating my badly-behaved, always-up-for-a-laugh image. The girls were sharing a cigarette on the field of the school during break-time, and I was watching them, thinking how endlessly cool it would be to be a smoker. They'd had, at most, a couple of drags each, when a teacher loomed on the horizon.

'Oh shit,' one of the girls said. 'Where are we going to put this?' She stubbed it out hurriedly on the grass and looked at me pleadingly.

'Don't worry,' I said gallantly, rising to the occasion, 'I'll hide it for you.'

I shoved the stub into the pocket of my school blazer where it sat for the rest of the day, giving me tantalising whiffs of stale cigarette smoke while I sat in lessons. I couldn't wait to smoke it, and enter into this new world I had a burning desire to become a part of.

That evening I hurried home, dumping my schoolbag in my room, and then ran downstairs, scavenging a handful of matches and tearing off a corner of the lighter paper from the side of the box.

'Matt, where are you off to?' shouted my mum as I scurried out the front door.

'Just meeting a friend quickly,' I mumbled back, darting down the road, not waiting for her to question me further. I squirrelled myself away under a streetlight in an alley near the house, and pulled out the cigarette butt, putting it in my mouth and lighting the first match. It went out immediately, the flame extinguished by the wind. I lit another, and the same thing

8

happened. And again. And again. I very quickly burnt through the entire handful of matches that I'd brought with me.

I didn't give up. Not when I'd come so close. I crept back to the house, and stashed another handful of matches in my pocket, before hurrying as quietly as I could back to my smoking spot. Finally, I managed to light the cigarette. I inhaled a few long drags, consumed by both the joy of smoking (and thus being officially cool) and the fear of being caught. I was very aware that one of my neighbours could come by at any moment and I had no doubt that they'd tell my parents what I'd been doing if they saw me.

I finished the cigarette and darted back into the house, scrubbing my teeth and covering myself with deodorant, heart pounding. Was it worth it? Absolutely. I was a smoker now.

Like almost everyone, I had to force myself to start, and then further push myself to have a habit. Weeks went by where I wouldn't have a cigarette; long, sulky summer holidays where I would park myself in front of the TV despite the heat of the Spanish sun outside. On returning to school I would scrabble together bits of change in order to buy cigarettes, and I'd begin again.

'Can I borrow 10p?' I'd ask my classmates, steadily and unashamedly working my way through them until I had 50p; the going price for one cigarette back then. That would be my only full cigarette of the day, and the rest of the time I would scavenge people's ends, sucking a few drags on a soggy second or third-hand cigarette.

Despite this inauspicious start, and my lack of money, by 14 I had a definite habit. This was helpful for my image and I didn't consider stopping until years later, after I'd been through rehab. It became a part of my identity, another layer of the Cool Matt, the untouchable persona I cultivated over the years. This is also when I first started selling cigarettes at school. I'd buy them from a friend's uncle, Barry, for £3 a pack and I'd flog them to my classmates, charging per ciggie. It was a lucrative business, which I carried on for many years.

***

My teenage years were also when first signs of drug use began creeping in, although this was nothing serious at the time. As a group of friends, we would often spend the evenings hanging around in the park, occasionally passing a joint between us, each of us just getting a few puffs. The first time I ever did this, the weed had very little effect on me. I remember stumbling around, pretending to act stoned, with no idea what being stoned looked or felt like. It was important to me, however, to keep being funny, and, as always, I was overjoyed that people were laughing at me.

This period of weed smoking was never anything problematic, and in fact it's a time in my life that I look back on fondly. Those evenings in the park were full of wide-eyed joy and the excitement of trying something brand new. We would release our inhibitions and talk about nothing and everything, once bursting into an impromptu group performance of The Lion Sleeps Tonight, harmonising and layering the vocals like we were in a Broadway performance of The Lion King. In hindsight, this cannot have been an impressive show. I cannot remember any of my friends being brilliant singers. But it felt amazing at the time. It was a golden period that I still talk about with the school friends I'm in touch with.

***

When I was 15, I was arrested for possession of weed. Again, this sounds much more dramatic and worrying than it was; although perhaps it was a sign of things to come. When it happened, it felt brilliant; my social status was elevated for a while afterwards, and I very much enjoyed the attention I got as a result.

The experience itself was actually, as you'd imagine, fairly stressful. I'd bought a quarter of weed from a friend at school, with the intention of selling part of it on to another friend, Mickey. We arranged to meet in Wymans Brook, just a minute's walk from my house. I stuffed the weed in my cigarette packet, stashing that in the inside pocket of my jacket. I couldn't be bothered to split it in two, figuring I'd do that when we met up. This turned out to be a very lucky decision; more than one bag of weed is an almost certain sign of dealing, and I could have got into much worse trouble than I did.

I left my house with my stash safely hidden away, and wandered down to the subway underneath the Windyridge Road, where Mickey and I had arranged to meet. I lit up a cigarette and leaned against the wall. It was a dingy area of Wymans Brook, and the subway was dank and musty smelling. I must have immediately looked suspicious hanging around there, but this wasn't something that even crossed my mind, even with the weed burning a hole in my pocket.

As I waited, I noticed two people – a man and a woman - cycling towards me. They looked like tourists, although why tourists would be hovering near a dirty subway, I wasn't sure. I made eye contact with one of them, but quickly looked away. I wasn't in the mood for conversation, or to be asked for directions to the centre of town.

As I craned my neck, looking around again for Mickey, I noticed one of the cyclists appearing at the other end of the subway, while the other circled round and began pedalling towards me again. They picked up speed and panic began to rise – was I being attacked? Mugged? Who were these people and what did they want from me?

Suddenly the man jumped off his bike and grabbed my arm, without introduction or explanation.

'What do you think you're doing here today?' he snapped. I freaked out. I still had no idea who these people were, or what was happening. Blank fear washed over me.

'What the fuck!?' I shouted – an instinctive reaction. I swung for the man in a panic, my hand lunging towards his face, physically shaking with fear.

'We're police,' he replied, dodging my punch, and tightening his grip on my arm, and suddenly it all clicked into place. Plain clothes police. Young male loitering by the subway. I suddenly felt terrified again, although for an entirely different reason.

'Do you have anything on you that you want to tell us about?' he said, 'it'll make your life easier if you tell us about it in advance.' They were both next to me now, leaning on their bikes and staring me down intimidatingly.

I did have something to tell them about, of course. I had £40 worth of weed that I was none too keen on giving away. On the other hand, I didn't want to go to prison for not complying with the police. Reluctantly I pulled out the cigarette packet where I'd hidden it and handed it over. *That's it*, I thought, *I can go home now*. I was seething, but didn't dare show it.

The policeman looked at the weed, and then glanced back at me.

'Anything else?' he asked and I shook my head.

'Nope, that's all,' I said, almost smugly. I knew I'd gotten away with it. There was a pause, and then the policeman's hand came down onto my arm again, his fingers wrapping around it as if to hold me in place.

'I'm arresting you for possession of a controlled substance,' he said, 'you don't have to say anything. But it may harm your defence if you do not mention, when questioned, something which you may later rely on in court. Anything you do say may be given in evidence.'

I felt my stomach drop, the adrenaline reeling inside me. I was gobsmacked. It felt surreal, like I was on a TV prank show. I looked around, searching for the cameraman, who surely any minute was going to jump out the bushes shouting SURPRISE. There was none – just Mickey, who saw the police, widened his eyes and swivelled, hurrying away rapidly. I didn't blame him.

I was transported to the police station in a riot van, not because I was an extreme danger, but because that was the only vehicle that they had available at the time. I was half enjoying myself by now, enough to appreciate the drama of the situation. Through the blacked-out windows of the van I could see an old friend from primary school in the car behind me, and I found myself wishing she could see me.

I became scared again when I got to the police station. I sat, knees drawn up, head on my legs in the cell, wondering what was going to happen to me now. I hadn't been told very much, just left in this blank and threatening room to wait. They'd taken all my personal belongings from me, including my shoes, and I felt small and frightened.

Suddenly the door clicked open, and there was the policeman and with him was my dad. That was the moment my heart really dropped, and I moved from stress into complete blind terror.

'I'll give you two a minute to chat,' said the policeman, and I remember thinking *no, NO! Please don't leave me with him!* He pulled the door shut as he walked away, and Dad took a step into the room quietly.

'How long have you been smoking weed?' he said, lowering himself onto the bench beside me.

'Once or twice, hardly ever,' I mumbled.

'Right, okay,' he said, deep in thought. There was a long pause, the silence so quiet I could hear my heart hammering. 'Well, we won't tell your mum'. I looked at him, but he was silent, his face shut down. The conversation was clearly over.

And that was it, really. I had an interview, where the police told my dad how responsible and co-operative I'd been. I was slapped with a caution and sent on my way, given a lift home with Dad in the same blacked-out riot van.

'Please drop us round the corner,' instructed Dad, clearly picturing the neighbours' faces as the two of us climbed out of such an ostentatious vehicle. His plan failed; as we pulled up, a gang of my friends saw me getting out the back, and began yelling excited questions at me.

'What's going on, Matt?' they screamed.

'Why are you in a riot van?'

'I'll catch you at home!' I shouted at Dad, as I raced away. I wasn't ready to face him yet.

When I crept home hours later, blood pumping fast at the thought of the confrontation, Dad was sat on the sofa waiting for me. He looked up at me as I came in, and I braced myself.

'Right, Matt,' he said, 'we won't tell your mum, and we'll never speak about it again'. And with that he levered himself off the sofa and headed upstairs. That was it.

Mum did find out, but only many years later, when I was confessing to her how bad my drug use had become.

'By the way, Mum,' I said, 'did you know that I was arrested for possession of weed when I was 15?' She didn't. And, of course, it hardly mattered by then. At the time though, it seemed like a very big deal - I felt famous. Being arrested had lifted me higher in people's estimations, and, for a short while, put me at the centre of attention. And that was what I really craved all along.

Chapter Two

Just a month after my arrest I was hit by a car, and narrowly escaped death.

I look back now on this accident, and it's so clear to me that this was a turning point in my life. The memories of what happened clung with me for a long time (and to some extent still do). My behaviour also changed afterwards; there was a permanent alteration to the way I felt about myself. If I hadn't been on the path to addiction before this day, I definitely was afterwards.

It was the 29th March 2008, and I was with my friend Aaron in Cheltenham. It was a Saturday, a miserable day, not quite raining, but spitting on and off. Aaron and I were killing time in the way we knew best in those days; smoking weed and chatting the day away.

We had crouched under a bridge a small way out of town to share a few single skins. We'd been hoping to avoid the rain, but then Aaron got a call from our friend Billy.

'Hiya mate,' he said, 'could I come and look through the stuff you've got in your skip?' Aaron had a huge house and his family were always doing projects and having clear-outs. The skips from these endeavours were a goldmine, and we all leapt at the chance to dig through them.

'Sure,' said Aaron, 'meet you at mine?'

Aaron lived in a place called Coombe Hill. Getting there involved a walk through Cheltenham, then a 40-minute bus ride, followed by a small trek along a busy main road. But still, even with the journey, it was better than our previous plans, so off we went, hoping that the rain would continue to hold out.

We got off the bus around an hour later, and began walking up the A38 towards Aaron's house. It was a single carriageway road, with a speed limit of 50mph, and there was no pavement, so we were wandering along the grass verge. I was still woozy from the weed, and talking nonsense to Aaron, who was just behind me. The cars were rushing past and I could feel their speed from where we were walking, and the shift in air pressure as they rushed past.

Billy's dad suddenly pulled up beside us in a van, with Billy and another friend, Joe, riding passenger.

'Is it up here lads?' he asked, waving at the road in front of us.

'Yep, it's that turning up there' I said, pointing at Aaron's driveway in the distance, 'we'll catch you up!'

It wasn't far, but we picked up speed, half-jogging, not wanting to be left out of the skip digging.

I was preparing to cross the road when it happened. I checked left and right, but somehow didn't see anything. I don't know how – a blind spot? Not checking properly? Either way, I stepped into the road – just one small step – straight into the path of an oncoming car.

'NO MATT, GET BACK!' screamed Aaron, but it was too late. I swivelled my head and saw the car looming towards me at what seemed like an incredible speed, the driver and the passenger wearing identical masks of shock. In a panic I ran forwards – further into the road.

There was a loud rev, impossibly close, like the engine was complaining about being dropped a gear. The faces of the driver and the passenger were clear to me now, and the passenger was clutching the driver like he was bracing himself for the inevitable.

And so did I. Some survival instinct kicked in, and I jumped as high as I could, curling my limbs into a ball to protect myself. My head smashed against the windscreen and I was thrown over the roof of the car. The noise was massive; a steely bang as the back of my head hit the glass.

And then, for a while, I was floating peacefully. I remember the sense of calm, paired with the awful realisation that I was going to die. My ears were ringing with a high-pitched beeping noise, and I could feel the blood coursing round my body with every beat of my heart. My parents came to me then, raising a glass to me, a vivid depiction of an old photo of them I'd had stuck up in my bedroom for years.

As I floated, thinking of my parents, I had an attack of conscience. Shit – I was dying – shouldn't I think about David too? To my relief, he came to me then, an image of him shuffling sideways through a door. It wasn't the clearest or best image of him I could have conjured, but I could die content in the knowledge that I'd had my whole family on my mind. I let myself go.

And then I woke up. I was lying in the middle of the road, with my arms still wrapped around my body. I slowly untangled myself and scrambled to my feet. The world felt strange, and my hearing was cloudy, like I was walking underwater. As my eyes met Aaron's I saw the vivid terror written all over his face, and I knew things were bad.

'A-Aaron,' I stuttered, 'I've j-j-just been h-h-hit by a car.'

'I know Matt,' he said, quietly, almost blankly, like he couldn't quite process what had happened.

I took a step towards him, suddenly hit with a powerful need to get out of the road and lie down.

'NO MATT, NO!' he shouted, an echo of his previous warning, and a van whizzed past me, just centimetres away. I could feel the air buffing against my face as it passed, and I could feel that something was wrong with me; the air felt colder than usual, and my skin began to sting.

Exhaustion hit me at that moment, and I felt my knees go weak. My brain had taken me past scared and into a vacant tiredness, and all I wanted to do was lie down and sleep.

The next few hours are a bit of a jumble in my memory. I was helped up to Aaron's house by Billy's dad and Joe, who had appeared – Aaron had apparently run all the way up to the house to get them, although I have no memory of this. My shoes had been blasted off by the impact of the car, and Billy had gathered them from where they'd been splayed on either side of the road. In a desperate attempt to be useful, he then scrabbled to put them on my feet as I staggered towards the house. I remember watching the blood drip from my face down to the shoes, and once again being hit by the knowledge that things were not okay, and that I was going to need some serious medical attention.

I finally caught a glimpse of myself in the mirror at Aaron's house as we went in, and the sight was horrifying. It looked like my face was hanging off. There was blood everywhere, dripping onto my clothes and clinging to my eyelashes. Nothing looked normal; it was a mash of exposed skin and pouring blood that looked nothing like my usual reflection. I glanced away quickly, feeling myself descending further into panic.

Aaron and his family parked me upright on their sofa, covering me in handfuls of tea towels which quickly became saturated with blood. There was a general sense of nervous energy in the room while we waited for the ambulance; everyone was desperate to do something, but no-one knew quite what to do.

Even in this time of great anxiety and pain, I still felt the need to be funny. I don't know why. Perhaps a learned coping mechanism, or a knee-jerk reaction to stress? Aaron's stepbrother came down the stairs and visibly balked at the sight of me.

'Whoa,' he said, reeling. 'WHOA. What is going on here?' I flashed him a cheesy grin despite the discomfort and fear.

'Bet you weren't expecting this when you came downstairs were you?'

Things got a lot scarier again when the paramedics finally arrived. There was a bit of confusion when they first bustled through the door.

'I thought you said he was hit at 60?' said one of them, looking at me perched upright on the sofa, alert, and strangely cheerful despite the circumstances.

'He was!' said Billy's dad. The ambulance crew paled.

'Why on Earth did you move him?' they said.

'He walked!'

'But… I thought you said he was hit at 60!?' It was clear to me that the fact I was still alive was amazing, and I felt very worried about what was ahead. Was I still in danger? What if I was bleeding out slowly? Was I going to die?

The ambulance crew laid me down on the living room floor, and put me into a neck brace, hooking various tubes into me for pain relief. As I was lying there on the floor, being attended to by several paramedics, the severity of what was happening to me hit me like a tidal wave and I panicked.

'Please don't let me die!' I said, repeating myself over and over. 'Please don't let me die, please don't let me die'. There were murmured reassurances, but the fear on the faces of everyone surrounding me told a different story.

I was wheeled out into the ambulance, the stretcher moving precariously over Aaron's gravel driveway. I wound my hands round the bars on the bed, terrified that the whole thing was going to jolt, and I was going to go crashing to the floor. It had started raining by now, and I felt the rain mix with the blood on my face and drip down into my eyes. It was almost a relief to get in to the warm safety of the ambulance.

I travelled to the hospital alone and terrified, watching my breath rise and fall in the fog of the oxygen mask that had been slipped over my face. We arrived at Cheltenham General and I was wheeled rapidly into A&E, where an entire response team was waiting for me, having been told only that a child had been hit at 60mph.

The commotion following my arrival was immense. The medical team were expecting someone who was clinging onto life, and were appropriately ready for any scenario. I remember the clamour and apparent chaos swirling around me, and how it made me fear for my life once more.

'I want my mum,' I whimpered, 'please don't let me die.'

'We'll call your mum, my love,' said a friendly nurse, rubbing my hand in an attempt to keep me calm.

'But she'll be worried, she watches Holby City!' I said, another joke flung in to make myself feel better. It worked. The nurses laughed and I felt more at ease.

To my relief, Mum did finally arrive shortly afterwards, tears streaming down her face, eyes searching me out across the A&E department.

'Hello Mum,' I said, trying my best to sound brave.

'Hello,' she said back, her voice thick with tears. I could see her fighting against her sobs, trying not to break down in front of me. I learned later how deeply traumatic this whole experience had been for her. She'd been reading a book when there had been a knock at the door.

'Hi,' said the man standing there, when she opened it, 'I'm a Family Liaison Officer. Can I come in? You might like to sit down.'

Mum's legs filled with jelly, and she felt unable to stand.

'I remember trying to get up the stairs to call your dad,' she said later, 'but I physically couldn't!'

My parents were told I had life-changing injuries. This was, of course, not true, but was a reasonable warning given what the emergency services knew about the accident at this point. My dad drove them to the hospital in the end; his way of clinging onto some semblance of control. I can't imagine how they must have felt, winding through the streets of Cheltenham in the early evening, not saying a word to each other, just trapped in their own silent panic. For years later, Mum was unable to read a book in the afternoon because of the memory of the Family Liaison Officer banging on the door. It must have been an awful time for both of them.

One by one the staff left the room I was in, everyone slowly realising that, at least medically, there was nothing wrong with me. I had various scans on various parts of my body, and all of them came back clear. I had some minor cuts and injuries, but apart from that I was, somehow, miraculously, absolutely fine. By the end of the evening, there was just me and a nurse left. My neck brace was finally removed and I was given a glass of orange juice with a straw, and a tuna mayo sandwich. I don't particularly like mayonnaise, so this was a hugely disappointing post-survival meal, an anti-climax after all that I'd been through.

I was transferred to the Gloucester Royal Hospital that night, as they wanted to keep me in for observation. I was still just under 16 at this point, so I needed to be admitted to a children's ward, and that meant a transfer. News of my accident had clearly spread among the medical community; I remember a doctor finishing his shift at Cheltenham and then driving to Gloucester just to lay eyes on 'the miracle boy'. I was indisputably lucky to be alive.

I had stitches in my face that night, which was by far the most painful part of the entire car crash experience. The anaesthetic injections were both hugely painful and entirely useless, and the whole stitching process took about an hour and a half. I sat there gritting my teeth for the entire time, clutching a nurse's hand as my face was sewn back together, stitch by agonising stitch.

The horror of the stitching was then followed by a truly awful night's sleep. I was on half-hourly observations, and any time I did manage to drop off I was woken by beeping, or tubes digging into me from some angle. I was exhausted, in pain and I couldn't get comfortable at all. By the time Sunday morning rolled around I couldn't wait to get away. I wanted to sleep in my own bed, and get out of the horrible noisy ward.

***

I was discharged from hospital about 24 hours after I was hit by the car; beaten up and shell-shocked, but alive and walking. It was a warm and sunny day, and Mum and Dad picked me up, all of us feeling slightly dazed about what had just happened.

'We're just going to nip into Gran's,' said Dad, as we drove home, the rumbling of the car beginning to lull me to sleep.

'Why?' I asked grumpily; I just wanted to get into bed and stay there.

'Because… well, because she wants to see you, Matt.' I nodded at this, suddenly understanding. It was obvious that she wanted to see with her own eyes that I was alive and (relatively) well.

We pulled up at Gran's, and my auntie came out to meet us. She was a theatre nurse, and had been for 25 years at that point. Even so, she stopped dead when she saw me, her hands flying to cover her mouth.

'Oh my God, Matt,' she whispered. I just shrugged. I was getting used to people looking horrified at this point.

We headed home shortly after, at my request. I was beyond tired, and just wanted to wallow and be looked after. As we drove down Windyridge Road, near to my house, I saw Joe, Billy, and Joe's girlfriend Stacey outside the local shop with a shiny gift bag and I felt a spark of excitement.

I'm coming home, meet me at mine, I texted them, turning my phone on for the first time that day. It was then that I saw how many people had been concerned about me; I had texts and missed calls in the hundreds. Despite the pain and the exhaustion, I suddenly felt completely happy.

From then on, I surfed a wave of popularity. Friends had to almost book appointments to come and see me, and I basked in the attention. Mum and Dad gave me free reign of the garage, and I sat in there for days, smoking as many cigarettes as I wanted, and being looked after by everyone around me.

Mum and Dad had to look after me physically as well; my body was still stiff and in shock from the impact, so I was helped around the house. Dad rubbed cream into my cuts three times a day, and I wasn't expected to lift a finger. I was coddled and fussed over and looked after more than I'd ever dreamed. I was living my dream life.

The trauma of the accident didn't hit me immediately. I remember actually enjoying the aftermath for a while; I felt like I was getting proof that everyone really did like me. This lasted for a few weeks; a first wave right after the accident, and then a second wave when I finally returned to school. I felt like a celebrity and I had no desire for it to end.

Eventually, though, my stitches were removed, and the attention I was getting began to fade. This was when I began to fade also, withdrawing into myself, and rejecting invitations or offers of company.

'Come for a smoke with us,' people would offer, and I'd shrug them off, their invitations irritating me. *They don't really care*, I thought to myself, *they don't want you there*. I'd had a glimpse of a life where I was the centre of attention at all times, and I'd loved it. I had no interest in returning to how things were before.

***

Trauma is a funny thing, and this accident took a long time to work its way to the surface. Years later, after I'd been to rehab, I braced myself and finally spoke about the effect it had had on me. I was in bits; tears and snot streaming down my face at the recollection of what I'd been through. For a long time, however, I buried this deep, brushing it off as an amusing anecdote.

'How did you get those scars, Matt?' people would ask me.

'Hit by a car, I was!' I would say, slamming my fist into my hand to mimic the impact. 'You should see the car, mate!'

I was, nevertheless, clearly traumatised, and struggling to deal with what had happened to me. The accident marked the start of a new period of my life; one where I was much more isolated. This is also when my drink and drug use began to gather speed, although it took a few years to get to a worrying level. What is undeniable is that things were never quite the same after the accident. I wasn't the same. Something had darkened within me, and it had begun to build.

Chapter Three

As I mentally pulled away from my friends, I sought solitude physically as well. School had become exhausting, and home was boring; I was desperate to find somewhere I could be alone and wallow in my thoughts. I wanted to be lonely so that I could feel sorry for myself; it was a self-inflicted abandonment.

This was when I began to go down to the stables, and so began another period of my life. I'd always been aware that the stables existed. They were derelict structures, long left to succumb to the weeds and the undergrowth. There was nothing much left of them, just the shells of the old buildings. I sometimes headed there with my friends to smoke weed and hang out on nice evenings. Now, confused by my own thoughts, and bitter after a brief period of popularity, it seemed like a good place to be alone.

That summer was hot, and it was long. I, and everyone in my year, had study leave in the run up to our GCSEs, and after that, months stretched out in front of me.

I would borrow what money I could from my mum and dad, and pick up a gram of weed. Hiding what I was doing, I'd roll a joint in my bedroom and then head down to the stables in the middle of the day when I knew no-one would be there.

I was in a bad mood for the entire summer. I was stuck between wanting everyone to pay me attention like they had after my accident, and also wanting to be alone. If friends did turn up at the stables asking if I was okay, I would push them away, while really feeling secretly overjoyed that they cared.

'Come on Matt,' they said when they found me there once. 'Why are you here alone? Come and have a smoke with us.'

'No, no, I'm fine,' I said, waving them away, refusing to even make eye contact. It made no sense to me at the time. Looking back, I was very much caught in a 'if I can't have everyone then I don't want anyone' mentality, traumatised and muddled-up over the accident, and my subsequent rapid rise and fall in popularity. At the time it was painful, and I felt angry at every single person in my life.

I was not always alone at the stables. Although the days were spent contemplating the world with no other company, every evening I would be visited by Pete on his way home from the factory. Even then, with little knowledge of addiction, I knew him as Pisshead Pete, and I could see the addictive routine in his days.

A factory worker who still lived with his mum, he would turn up at 6pm on the dot. He was an imposing figure, menacing and large, with a bald head, always trailing cigarette smoke behind him. He carried a tote bag with him, in which he kept a DVD player, a small radio, a glass and eight cans of Strongbow.

'Matthew,' he'd say to me to acknowledge my presence.

'Cushty Pete,' I'd say, a Cheltenham way of greeting people. I was always thrilled that he was acknowledging me, but I never showed it. I always played it very cool with Pete, hiding how much I admired him.

Pete would settle himself down on the old armchair he kept down there, and I'd watch him, fascinated by his nightly ceremony. First, he'd pull out a bag of ice, which he'd drop on one of the concrete blocks to smash. He'd then wipe his glass, shove a few handfuls of ice in it, pour his drink and settle himself in his chair. He'd pick a film from the selection of DVDs he had with him, and then he'd light a cigarette and start drinking.

I loved this. I loved the habit, the calm ritual of the process, and I loved being a tiny part of it. As the summer drew on, I stopped going to the stables so much in the day, and started joining Pisshead Pete every evening. I'd clock-watch at home all day and then barrel down there at 5:30 so I'd be there in time to watch Pete do his thing.

I got bored of the cannabis around this time also. It wasn't fun anymore, and it felt lonely and sad. Instead, I began drinking. I was 16 by now, and I was still putting on a face to my parents, who were convinced I had a thriving social life.

'I'm off to a party tonight, Dad!' I would say, 'Can I have a bottle of Strongbow?'

I hated the taste of alcohol, but I loved the buzz it gave me, and I could just about stomach cider. Dad would buy me a big bottle, allegedly for sharing round at the 'party', although in reality it was just me drinking it on my own. It didn't fit in the fridge at home, so I would swig it lukewarm, straight from the bottle. Being like Pete was important to me, and I took a strange sort of pride in flinging my empty Strongbow bottle onto the rising mountain of his discarded cans. I appreciated the kindness he showed me, and the way he enjoyed having me there. It was a very strange friendship, but it served both of us, sat together in our needy bitterness, hating the world.

'I only trust two people in this world, and that's my mum and you, Matthew,' he would say to me, and I'd smile at the compliment, and at the feeling of being needed.

My parents never knew about our friendship, and I didn't want them to know. It was a part of my life that I enjoyed very much, but I knew deep down that there was something strange about it; something weird and shameful.

One night, the doorbell rang while I was home. Mum opened the front door, and I got a glimpse of Pete's bald head in the doorway, his frame looming over her as they spoke. The feeling of worry was huge. What was he doing here? What was he saying to my mum? Why?

It turned out not to be Pete. It was one of Mum's friends who was similar in stature, and had the same bald head. Still, my desire to keep the friendship private intensified. I never once told him where I lived, and never told any of my other friends that I was spending time with him. It was my secret, and it was important that it stayed that way.

I would go to the stables as often as I could. Pisshead Pete and I could be found there whatever the weather, huddled up in layers in the winter, sheltering from the drizzle when it rained. Pete brought scrap pieces of wood from the factory and we burned them in the corner, coughing with the smoke, the cold still penetrating through. To explain the smell of smoke, I told my parents that there were always bonfires at the parties.

'Sounds fun, Matt,' they said.

Occasionally, on a Friday or Saturday night, Pete would pull out his phone and make a call.

'You about mate?' he would say, cutting straight to it. There would be a pause in the conversation, and then, 'yeah usual place.' He'd hang up, and disappear into the hedges that surrounded the stables, coming back with a small lump of white powder wrapped in cling film.

I was mesmerized by this process. I would ask to look at the cocaine, rolling the small ball of cling film between my fingers, amazed at being so close to something so illegal and so cool. I'd stare at Pete as he unpicked the wrapper, crushed up the coke with his DVD case and then did a line in front of me, huffing it up his nose with a rolled-up note.

There was never any pressure for me to do it. In fact, it was almost the opposite – Pete was very protective of his cocaine, and never offered to share. Nonetheless, after a few weeks of watching him, the curiosity got too much. Pete never seemed any different after a line, and I was desperate to know what it felt like.

One night, I plucked up the courage to ask him.

'Can I have a go, Pete?' I muttered nervously. Pete was still a little intimidating to me, and our strange friendship hadn't crossed this line yet.

There was a pause.

'Alright, Matthew,' he said finally, and cut up two lines instead of one.

He helped me to do that first line, guiding me through the process, and telling me exactly what to do.

'Hold one nostril shut,' he told me, 'and breathe in through the other. It's not rocket science.'

I did as I was told, sniffing that line up, and then standing up again. Pete was looking at me with a huge cheesy grin on his face, nodding his head in approval.

That night, we watched a film as usual, then sat back and listened to the radio. At around 10 we headed home, like we did on any night. I felt normal, just with a slightly blocked nose, but it wasn't about the effect on me, not then. It was about the status. I felt like I was part of a big and scary club now, and I had every intention to stay.

After that, I did cocaine whenever I was able. Pete was very stingy – he never gave me more than one or two little lines. Occasionally I'd manage to scrimp and save up £20 and we'd go halves. The drugging was never uncontrollable when I was with Pete; I was just an occasional recreational cocaine user. I felt accepted and part of something big; 'one of the lads' in a way I'd never felt before.

This feeling of having entered a new and more exciting club was reinforced whenever one of Pete's friends came down to spend time with us at the stables. They were an assortment of weird characters, and all of them remain vivid in my memory.

There was Geoff, who came down every night for a while, and smoked cannabis through a bong. He'd inhale the smoke like he was smoking a pipe, and then, in a stoned fog, he would talk to us about communism or religion. He was an incredibly intelligent man, but clearly a loner; his evenings were spent at home in his mum's house painting Warhammer figurines.

Bobby Compton also lived with his mum, flicking from job to job. He was a compulsive liar, and used to get so caught up in his tangled web of untruths that he'd begin to believe them himself.

'I just found a briefcase with £10,000 in it!' he'd exclaim, and we'd all nod as if we'd heard it all before. Mainly because we had.

Bobby hated me; we'd had a fight when I was around 16, purely because he was 23 at the time and thought I was an easy win. Unfortunately for him, that backfired. My memories of what exactly happened are blurry, but I won the fight, and from then on, Bobby held a grudge. He'd glower at me from his corner of the stables, as if he wanted to challenge me to a rematch, but didn't quite dare.

Bobby also had a sidekick, a quiet man called Peanut. He never said a word, just sat with Bobby as if for moral support, nodding at every word he said. Bobby and Peanut were well known for their stealing; they would regularly scour the local area looking for pushbikes to swipe and sell on for cheap.

There were numerous other characters who would come down to smoke a joint with us; Big Chris, Kipper and others, a bizarre collection of odd men with strange nicknames. I just looked on in awe and amusement, fascinated by it all. It felt like being part of a sitcom, and I felt privileged to be there witnessing it all.

This period at the stables definitely cemented some of my future. I looked up to Pete, and I very much wanted to be like him. I couldn't think of anything I'd enjoy more than working a factory job and then spending my evenings drinking and drugging before going home for a takeaway. It never occurred to me that this was a lowly ambition, or that I could do better for myself. This was what I wanted, and to some extent I set my heart on it from then on.

***

My lack of ambition showed in my GCSE results. They were fine. Perfectly adequate. Exactly what you'd expect from someone who was relatively intelligent, but smoked weed before several of his exams; Bs, Cs and a few Ds. This worked out fine for me. It was enough to get into Sixth Form, and going to Sixth Form was enough for me to put off getting a job for another few years, and therefore enough to get my mum off my back.

I had still been popular in school towards the end of my GCSEs, but once I started Sixth Form everything changed. I transferred to Cleeve, as Pittville didn't have a Sixth Form. With the bus stop just a minute's walk from my house, it was by far the easiest option. Most of my mates, all with a more ambitious spirit than me, had gone to work in various trades, and so I was suddenly left alone. I felt very alone as well. I spent the vast majority of my time smoking down the passageway we called Fag Alley, or skipping lessons to drink in the pub.

My main focus during these final two years at school was on getting money so I could buy drink and drugs at the weekend. I was still selling cigarettes, but I was now able to buy them myself. I wasn't actually old enough yet, but I was tall, and in Sixth Form we didn't have to wear a school uniform. I was never asked for ID. My cigarette business was getting me reasonable money; sometimes as much as £20 a day, an absolute fortune for a schoolkid. With my earnings in hand, I'd then head to the pub in my free periods, weaving back to catch the bus home at the end of the day. I was quite often a spectacle on the way home, singing Elvis tunes at the top of my voice to the bemusement of everyone around me.

This description makes it sound like I was completely friendless, but that's not true. Sometime during Sixth Form I began hanging out with another group of friends, who were from neither school, and we spent a lot of time together. For the life of me I cannot remember how we met, but I do remember that our relationships revolved heavily around drink. I'd moved on from Strongbow to neat vodka, simply because the taste of alcohol still made me feel a bit sick and I didn't have to drink as much vodka to get completely hammered. And of course, getting completely hammered was the aim.

This descent into heavy drinking got me in trouble eventually. I'd reconnected with an old friend from primary school, Leon, and I tagged around with him at school despite us having nothing in common. I did crave company at times, despite my stony exterior, and Leon was better than nothing. He was also, unfortunately, a gossip and a shit-stirrer, someone who absolutely thrived off causing drama.

'You know that Nick?' he said to me once on a night out, pointing at a mutual friend in the street.

'What about him?' I asked, squaring up already. I'd had almost an entire bottle of vodka to myself, and was feeling riled-up and angry.

'He's told me he wants to batter you mate.' In hindsight this was clearly an exaggeration, and I should have known better than to immediately believe Leon. At the time, I saw red. By the time Nick approached us later in the night, I was both seething and very, very drunk.

'Alright mate,' he said to me.

'You wanna fight me then do ya?' I snapped straight back at him, gunning for some conflict.

'No, not really…' he said, clearly confused. I swung a punch anyway, and missed, swirling my fist out into thin air. I was so wasted I was completely unprepared for what happened next, and before I knew it, I was on the ground, my head being slammed into the kerb by his foot.

Nick kicked me several times, making sure I knew my place, and I wouldn't come after him again. He then ran away and I staggered up, helped unenthusiastically by Leon.

'Why didn't you help?' I roared at him, now angry beyond reason.

'I dunno,' he said nervously. That wasn't good enough. I swung for him as well, making contact this time, and sending him flying into a park bench, before storming off.

I was so angry I did the only thing I knew what to do; I drank another 35cl bottle of vodka. By the time I got home I was catatonic, the mixture of concussion and vodka causing me to throw up again and again and again.

This event had two fairly significant effects. One, it made me more isolated. The tiny grain of support I had from Leon in school was now gone, and I was actively hated by him and his group of friends. Two, I'd made the connection between pain relief and alcohol. I hadn't felt a thing while I was being battered, and I made a note of this in my head.

I went straight back to the stables to do my drinking after that, even more unhappy than I'd been before. I dreaded going to school and by the time my A-Level exams came around I was more than ready to leave education.

I failed my exams of course. Well, I say I failed my exams, but I don't actually know. I just never picked up my results. They're almost certainly still gathering dust in the bowels of the school to this day.

'Your parents will get a fine if you don't turn up to the exam, Matt,' my teachers told me, and so I turned up half pissed, scrawled my name on the top of the paper and promptly fell asleep on the desk.

No one was surprised by my lack of effort. The teachers had long since given up on me, and, like with my GCSEs, my parents were expecting nothing less. There was no concern though. Despite my unhappiness and lack of ambition, I was now well practiced at putting on a mask and appearing content.

***

I lasted about a month at home doing nothing before Mum and Dad put their foot down.

I'd been happily stalling them for a while, applying for jobs around Cheltenham and then deliberately flunking the interviews. I had no intention of working, and I was perfectly happy with my life as it was.

Unfortunately, my parents had other ideas. Dad stocked the papers at the local shop on a Saturday and Sunday morning, and he had a quick word with the manager one day.

'Sally, would you please give my boy a job?' he asked, pretty much begging. I was becoming a real annoyance at home, and I clearly wasn't going to get myself out of this.

'Anything for you, Mike!' Sally beamed. My dad is a charming man, reliable and a hard worker, and she had no reason to think that his son would be anything less. Unfortunately for her, she hadn't figured out the link between Sweet and Charming Mike, and the little stoner who used to hang around the local shop. I'd never been rude or abusive towards her, but she saw me as a bit of a waste of space, a loveable rogue who did nothing but eat Belgian buns and waste time.

I wandered into the shop a few days later and saw her stacking shelves.

'Any chance of a job Sally?' I yelled cheerfully and she just laughed.

'Not a chance,' she scoffed back at me, a perfectly reasonable response given my reputation. I scoffed right back at her.

'I'm Mike's son!' I announced, pulling out my trump card. She went visibly white.

'Oh my God what have I done?' she muttered, ushering me into the back.

I wasn't expecting to get a job. I planned to do the same as in every other interview; slump, answer monosyllabically, and generally make my lack of commitment known. This wasn't to be.

'Right,' said Sally, 'you've got a job, but here's how it's going to go...'

I was horrified. I had no chance of flunking this interview, because there wasn't one! I was talked through my role and my responsibilities, my working hours, the rules of the job, how much I'd be paid, how long my breaks were, and what my shift

patterns would be. There was no chance to even say yes or no –
I was in.

Chapter Four

Despite the reluctant start I found that I hugely enjoyed working at the shop. I didn't do many hours a week, just four, or sometimes five days, but I was suddenly earning steadily and reliably for the first time in my life. I was getting around £700 a month and I had barely any outgoings, so I was left with more disposable income than I'd ever had before. Most of this went on booze and drugs and clothes, and that was truly all that I wanted. I felt like I'd achieved success and I was completely happy with where I was.

It wasn't just the money that was making me happy; the job itself was perfect for me, and I soon settled into a happy new routine. I rapidly became well-known for my cheery and cheeky demeanour, and I was beloved by the regulars. I'd stand at the tills, bantering with the local little old ladies about their husbands and their breakfasts, their pets and their knitting, the perfect combination of caring and cute. If a line formed, I'd ring the bell for another checkout supervisor, and there would be a disgruntled sigh from the line in front of me.

'We'll just wait here for Matt's till!' they'd say, patiently queuing up for their spot with me. For someone who thrived on interaction with and attention from other people, this was perfect. It was exactly what I wanted from a job, and I'd come happily into work every shift, looking forward to the day ahead.

Management also loved me, and I had them wrapped around my little finger. The banter was constant; the managers and I would shout at each other up and down the aisles, having raging arguments with an undercurrent of mutual respect.

'Matt, would you stack the shelves?' Sally would say, clicking in her heels down the aisle, frazzled by the disorganisation in the store.

'Course, Sal,' I'd reply, with no intention of doing anything other than standing and chatting to customers.

Once, during a particularly busy shift, Jackie, one of the supervisors, approached me.

'Matt,' she said, 'could you have a look at the milk for me?'

'Sure thing, Jackie!' I said cheerfully. I headed towards the fridges, and stood in front of them. They were basically empty; just one or two bottles of milk remained. *Well*, I thought to myself, *I've looked at the milk.*

Shortly afterwards I heard Sally talking to Jackie.

'The fridge is completely empty, Jackie,' she said.

'I asked Matt to do it!' came the response. Sally approached me where I was lurking in the warehouse, doing my best to look busy.

'Matt, did Jackie ask you to check the fridges?'

'Yeah,'

'And did you?'

'Yeah,'

'And did it need refilling?'

'Yeah,'

'Well go and fucking do it then!' she yelled. The warehouse erupted in laughter, and I felt amazing. I knew that everyone hoped for a laugh when I was on shift, and I was pretty much guaranteed to deliver.

Before long, management and I reached a happy compromise, and I was put on the tills full time. This suited me perfectly. In quiet times I would stand there reading the newspaper, and when it was busy, I would throw myself into work. I was more contented than I'd been in a long time.

***

My social life also began to thrive once I started working at the shop. I began to make the transition between sulking down at the stables with Pete and going out partying in town.

The 2010 World Cup was on that summer, and I leapt on every single match as an excuse to hit the town. I'd be there at every game without fail, no matter who was playing, no matter what time it was on. I hated football, and still do, but I was lured to the pub by the crowds and the drinks deals. I would be the only person not watching the football, but I didn't mind. I'd face the crowds, swigging on my £1 pint, cheering on whoever was playing without a care in the world.

I had actually started going to town with Pete initially. He ventured out once in a while to join some of his friends in their own territory, but soon went back to the comfort of the stables. The atmosphere in town lured me in, however, and I was soon spending time with Pete's friends without him there. It was like he'd handed over the baton to other people and his mates began to look out for me.

The more I partied in town, the more I hung around with people who were regulars on the Cheltenham nightlife scene. They were friends of friends of friends of Pete and the people he knew, and many of them had a dark reputation that followed them. As I went deeper into their world, I realised that they were heavily involved in the crack cocaine and heroin underbelly of Cheltenham, and many were dealers. They hung around the pubs and bars I went to with several phones and wads of cash. This should have put me off, but it didn't – if anything, it excited me. I wasn't stupid enough to want to be a part of that world (yet, anyway), but I was image-conscious enough to want the reputation that went with it.

I began spending a lot of time with Vinnie Slater. He was well-known around Cheltenham; a walking ASBO with a reputation for violence and general criminal behaviour. Despite this, and despite his general air of roughness, Vinnie took me under his wing that summer. He was always good to me, looking after me on raucous nights out. Fuelled by booze and cocaine, I'd get into ridiculous fights, knowing that if things got too rough, Vinnie would step in and rescue me. It was a good feeling, this sense of being untouchable, and it definitely gave me more confidence than I had earned.

One night, Vinnie and I were walking down the street, when we saw two policemen coming from the opposite direction. We were blurry with drink and overly confident as a result, and Vinnie raised a hand in greeting at them as we passed.

'Hello Vinnie,' said one of them warily, 'who's your mate?'

'This is Matthew,' said Vinnie, slapping me on my shoulder in pride. He called me Matthew just like Pisshead Pete did. I puffed my chest up and nodded at the police. I was hoping they took notice.

A few weeks later I was out with other friends, when the same policemen headed towards us.

'Evening, Matthew,' they said, nodding at me cheerfully. I was delighted.

'Yeah, they know I'm trouble,' I bragged to my mates, lying through my teeth, but feeling their admiration wash over me. It had the desired effect. I began to get a reputation.

Slowly, the stables began to fade out of my life completely, replaced by partying with my new friends. I didn't miss it. My new life was much more exciting, and infinitely more fun. Pete missed me though. He became very jealous, and he made several attempts to guilt trip me into spending time with him again. He'd send me texts about how I didn't care anymore, and he'd pick his ice up at the shop when I was on shift, asking me if I was coming to the stables.

I began to make excuses.

'Nah, not tonight, Pete, I'm working,' I'd say, both of us knowing I wasn't. I'd see him walking back from the stables while I was in the pub, and I'd hide, cowering behind a wall as he peered through the window. Over time he stopped looking in, and then he stopped walking past the pub completely. I would like to say that I felt bad about this, or that there was a twinge of pity for him, but that would be a lie. In reality, he just faded from my thoughts and I moved on with my life.

I did go down to the stables one final time, a few months later. It was a warm evening, and I was skint, as I often was back then. I bought myself ten cans and plodded down there to kill some time, hoping for a warm welcome and some attention, without having to spend any money.

Pete all but refused to speak to me. I drank a few cans in a painfully awkward silence, making strained attempts at conversation. It was going nowhere.

'See ya then, Pete,' I said, packing the remainder of my cans into my bag. I walked away up the track, leaving the stables behind for good.

I saw Pete a few times again, walking down the road on his way to or from the stables. We would acknowledge each other awkwardly, but we never reached that level of friendship again.

Those times in the stables had been left in the past. The door had slammed shut on them, and I didn't look back.

Years later, just a few months before I went to rehab, I was driving my shiny BMW around Cheltenham when I saw him. I hit the brakes and rolled the window down.

'ALRIGHT PETE!' I yelled at him, waving madly. I wanted the man who'd given me my first line of cocaine to see what an admirable and enviable person I'd become. Image was everything to me at that point, and on some level, I still cared what he thought. He smiled vaguely in my direction, but that was all.

I've heard that he is still trapped in the same routine. The stables were demolished, but he still takes his Strongbow somewhere every night, and sits and drinks next to his radio. I went on to wreak havoc and destruction. Pete just seems to never get any better or any worse; truly a slave to his routine.

Now, I think fondly of him, this gentle man who showed me kindness when I was very low. I wish him nothing but peace and happiness.

***

I tried pills for the first time that summer of 2010, just for the sake of it. Anything that would get me wasted was something I was willing to give a go, especially something that would keep me awake, and therefore keep the party going.

It was Barry who sold them, the same Barry who'd sold me cigarettes cheap so I could flog them at Pittville School. I'd sidle up to him in the pub, give him £1.50, and he'd give me a little pill from his top pocket. We'd then both shuffle away without really speaking to each other. I loved the drama of it, and, of course, I loved the feeling of the drugs themselves.

These were golden times. I'd party until 6 or 7am, then stagger home, belting out songs at the top of my lungs into the rising sun. I was the karaoke king, always singing Elvis songs in the pubs, surrounded by friends cheering me on. I had the balance right between alcohol and cocaine, and I never felt rough the next day. I would spring out of bed on a few hours' sleep and jump straight into work at the shop, flirting with customers all day.

My parents had no reason to worry, and they didn't.

'I've had loads of sleep,' I'd say as I ran out the door to work, and they believed me. My tiredness at home was just put down to me being busy; I was working a lot on top of my social life after all.

I felt at times like I was living a double, if not triple, life. I was grumpy and withdrawn with my parents, sulky, and with no time for them. In the daytime I turned on the charm at work, and then at night I was partying heavily, downing drinks and hanging around with drug dealers.

Still, I was happy, really happy. These truly were the glory days, and I felt like I could keep up forever.

***

This period of my life was when I met Debbie, or Deb as she preferred to be known. She used to come into the shop every day with her husband, Phil, and occasionally her brother, Harry, all of them stocking up on vodka and cigarettes for the day ahead. This was another friendship that shaped my future, planting ideas and behaviours in my head that helped carry me down the road I was already on.

It should be apparent by now that I was propelled through life by a complete lack of ambition; my dream was to do utterly nothing, and Deb and Phil were living the life I aspired to live one day. They barely worked, living on the tail ends of a huge redundancy payment, and spent their days drinking at home. What more could anyone want?

I felt a kinship with Deb from pretty much the first time she set foot in the shop, and she often invited me to go and drink with them. I never went - I felt too awkward to accept their invitation. It was a number of months later, when they helped me out of some serious hot water, that we became good friends.

It started with a trip into town one night with a load of mates and a decision to go to a nightclub. This was a standard night out; we were very drunk, and desperate to let off some steam by seeing what trouble we could find.

The entry fee to the club was an expensive £7, but I coughed up the cash without complaint, and headed in. I was making my way up towards the music when suddenly I heard a shout from the doorway.

'Matt,' a mate said, waving me back down, 'we can't get in!'
I stomped back down the stairs.

'Excuse me, could I have my entry fee back?' I asked the bouncer, 'I'm not going in if my friends aren't.'

'No sorry mate, you have to go in, now,' I was told. I looked at the bouncer in disbelief.

'Really?' I asked, my voice flickering with annoyance.

'Yep, those are the rules I'm afraid, mate.'

'Fine,' I snapped. Snapped in every sense. I stormed back up the stairs, all logic gone from my brain. There was a huge mirror hanging on the wall on the stairs that led up to the dancefloor, and I attacked it. I smashed it with my fists at first, and then kicked it, holding onto the bannisters so I could ram both legs into it at full force.

The mirror came crashing down, and in the chaos that ensued I charged up the stairs and quickly ran into the club, pulling out all the light fittings as I went.

I darted onto the dancefloor, ducking behind people in order to keep myself hidden. *Fuck, Matt, calm down*, I thought to myself, *have a drink and just calm the fuck down.*

I downed a drink, the alcohol warming me and having the desired effect. I felt calmer, my breath slowing down and my heart settling. Much calmer in fact. I wandered out into the smoking area, fishing round for my cigarette packet and beginning to enjoy myself.

Suddenly, I felt a hand on the scruff of my neck, and I was dragged unceremoniously outside to where my mates were all still hanging around. Three bouncers surrounded me so I had no chance of running, and the police turned up, my friends going nowhere, all clamouring at the excitement.

'Let him go!' one of them screamed, despite having no idea what I'd done. This was the sort of drama we all thrived on, and everyone was enjoying the performance in some ways, including me.

I was let go that night, promising that I'd come back and pay £1000 for the damages.

'Absolutely,' I said, relieved I was being let off, 'I'll be back first thing tomorrow.'

I wasn't. I was lying through my teeth. In fact, I left the country, going on a day trip to Belgium to pick up cheap cigarettes with Barry. I was paid in cigarettes for just being a passenger, and it seemed like the perfect time to get away for the day. I had a Strongbow and a lasagne on the ferry, and stared out at the waves, trying not to think about the police and the nightclub.

I turned my phone on that evening when the ferry docked back in the UK. I was flooded with missed calls and voicemails; it was like when I'd been hit by the car, except much less positive. These were all from the police asking where I was, and threatening to arrest me.

I panicked. For the first time ever, I genuinely had no idea what to do; Mum and Dad were on holiday at the time, and there was absolutely no-one to bail me out. I spent the drive back to Cheltenham in silent stress, trying and failing to think of a plan of action.

We pulled up next to the shop, and Deb, Phil and Harry were there.

'Alright Matt?' said Deb, grinning at me.

'Fuck no,' I replied, blurting out the situation I was in. It was a relief to get it out.

'Give me the bouncer's number, Matt,' said Harry, 'I'll sort it for you. No worries.'

I handed him my phone, unable to believe my luck. With one short phone call the fine had been reduced to £100, which I had to pay tomorrow in cash. There was obviously something dodgy going on, but that wasn't my problem. I felt almost weak with gratitude.

I went to Deb and Phil's house for the first time that night, in celebration of my lucky escape. We sat at the kitchen table drinking vodka and playing cards, smoking the cheap cigarettes I'd brought back from Belgium.

That was the first time of many. I became a regular feature at their house in the evenings, often joined by Harry, who seemed to drift in and out of Deb's life at random. It was another new group of friends and, once again, I had that settled feeling of being loved and accepted.

41

Looking back now, it seems obvious to me that I was being used. Deb had been given a £35,000 redundancy payment, and though they'd lived off that for a while, it was close to gone. They were scraping by with money from Phil's dodgy back-room tattoo business, and the odd bit of beauty therapy that Deb managed to do. Ultimately, however, they were really struggling for money. When I came round, I always provided the booze, and, as such, they were always happy to have me.

At the same time, it's possible that I was using them in some ways. I only went round to Deb's when I was skint; the rest of the time I would go pubbing or clubbing in town. It was like a replacement for the stables in some ways; a bolthole when I was low on cash, but when I still wanted company and alcohol.

Nevertheless, Deb and I rapidly formed a strong friendship. She called me her 'little brother' (despite a 20-year age gap), and we became extremely close. We'd tell each other everything, and we provided each other with support as we navigated life.

Phil was more difficult to please.

'I only care about one person,' he'd say, 'and that's my wife'. Despite this, he'd welcome me in with open arms when I turned up with a bottle of vodka. I had some really fun times in that house, despite Phil's reluctance. We'd often talk the night away, playing game after game of cards, and laughing into the small hours of the morning. The house felt like a zoo at times; Deb had a whole collection of animals, but it was always clean and tidy, and I felt welcomed and safe there.

After I'd been working at the shop for about eighteen months, Deb got a job there too. I was thrilled; what could be better than working with my best mate? I was sure that work was going to get even better from now on.

I was right. It was the best fun I'd had since starting. Deb and I would schedule our drinking around our shifts, getting lunch at the Slug and Lettuce and sometimes forgetting to eat, downing pint after pint instead. We'd often roll into work drunk and giggling, slurring as we served customers, sniggering as we swayed on our feet.

These were the best times at the shop. My drinking was amusing, and my colleagues and even the customers would just laugh if I rolled in pissed. The managers weren't exactly happy, but I was doing my job, and doing it well, and that was all that mattered. I had £700 in my pocket each month, and drinking to do every weekend. It felt like life couldn't get any better.

Deb was another strange friendship, but again, it was a relationship that served me well at the time. We very much enjoyed spending time together, and during this happy and almost carefree period of my life she was someone I aspired to be like. I had never had a friend like her.

Chapter Five

What goes up must come down, and before long I began to struggle with my lifestyle.

Money was still coming in from my work at the shop, but I began to spend far more than I could afford, splashing out on drugs and booze at every opportunity, with very little thought about the consequences. I was often to be found scrabbling desperately for cash before payday.

One night at the pub, with almost no money left to keep me going until payday, I had a go on the fruit machine for the first time. I fed my final £1 into it, hoping for the best. *What do I have to lose?* I thought. Luckily, or perhaps unluckily, I won the jackpot on my first go, a £70 pay-out. I'd been skint when I went to the pub, so the win felt incredible; I surfed the high for a while.

That single fruit machine experience kicked off another huge problem for me; gambling. I chased that first fruit machine high from then on, losing money over and over in pubs, often head-butting machines in a rage when all my cash disappeared. As is the way with gambling, I lost far more often than I won, and before long I had simply added another expensive habit to the list.

I began to borrow from my parents, from friends, from random people in the pub, all to keep up with my habits. I was always skint, in debt, or both.

Luckily for me, I had some savings. Trevor had been regularly giving both me and my brother £100 for Christmas and £50 for birthdays and my parents had been diligently paying this into a savings account for us. By the time I remembered it, the amount was at nearly £2000, and there was nothing my mum could do to stop me withdrawing it.

'Please Matt, don't spend it all,' begged Mum. She knew me well, and she could see where this was going to go. I took it anyway.

I loaned £500 to Deb and Phil. Deb wanted some equipment to start up a beauty business, and Phil needed more tattooing gear. They did repay me, I feel I need to say that, but very, very slowly. They'd give me tiny bits of cash, or tempt me round to theirs with the promise of a 'free night', which just meant that they would provide the alcohol. It took a long time to get the money back, by which time I'd all but forgotten about it.

After I'd loaned Phil and Deb their money, I spent the rest within a week, splashing it around on unnecessary treats for myself, and piles of drugs and booze. With all my savings gone, I needed more.

This was when I got sucked in by payday loan companies, and the allure of fast cash. The first time I used a payday loan company was with Deb and Phil. An advert flicked onto the TV, and my eyes lit up; it seemed like the perfect solution to my problems. As long as I could afford to pay it back on payday then all would be fine – and payday was so far away!

We were all at it in the end, Deb, Phil and I, maxing out on payday loans from every company we could find. As long as we had enough for a bottle of vodka that night then everything was okay, and the tangled knot of financial difficulty we were weaving could wait for another day.

Whenever things got bad, I'd find a way to work myself out of the situation. Sometimes I'd just borrow more, finding some obscure payday loan company that I'd not used before, or borrowing from the bank. Occasionally someone different would lend me money and I'd be able to scrape together enough to keep me on my feet.

I sold my CD collection at one point, unable to think of any other way to get cash. This remains one of my greatest regrets. I'd been collecting CDs since I was about 10 years old, scrabbling together my pocket money to get one every month if I could. At one point, my collection had been my pride and joy; I would dust them carefully, and rearrange them. I must have spent hundreds of pounds on them all over the years, and I had never once dreamed of parting from them.

But then, needing money urgently, that changed. I was at Deb's house when I saw an advert for a CD buying company on the TV. Just scan your CDs and pop them in the post, and you'll have the cash in no time, it promised. I bit. I scanned every single one of those CDs, and hit sell, raising a whopping £27. I then went straight to my mum.

'Look Mum, I'll have £27 in a few days. Can I borrow it now and I'll pay you back?' I showed her the receipt on my phone, and looked at her eagerly.

Reluctantly, she agreed, and I headed straight down to the pub feeling rich. Of course, it was all gone in just a couple of hours, and I was borrowing again by the end of the night. By the time I posted off my CDs I had absolutely nothing to show for it. It was a truly miserable feeling, and I felt genuinely remorseful as I went to the Post Office. I have Spotify now, and access to any music I want, but I still miss my collection in some ways. It was a real childhood achievement, and there were many memories in those discs. If I could get them back, I would.

I'd often turn to my parents for cash. Despite not knowing the full extent of the situation, every time things got terrible, they'd bail me out financially. I only went to them when things seemed impossible; they never had much money themselves, and despite my selfish spending and reckless attitude towards life I was very aware of this. Nevertheless, I was bailed out by my poor mum on more than one occasion.

And then, of course, I'd start all over again.

Part of this attitude towards money was inherited from Deb and the way she treated her finances. I am in no way blaming her for the decisions I made, however, hanging around with her and observing her spending habits planted certain ideas in my head.

Firstly, she didn't value money. She'd spend anything she had almost immediately, and then live on almost no food until she got paid again. I followed suit. In my mind, money was there to be spent, not saved. The thought of putting anything aside never entered my head, and I spent all I had, and then more.

Secondly, the way Deb blew her £35,000 redundancy payment like it was normal planted a seed in my head. When I received a huge amount of money later down the line, I barely considered doing anything with it except spending it all. We'll get to that of course, but it's important to acknowledge how much my relationship with Deb affected my thinking.

***

Enter MCAT. Mephedrone, also known as drone, or White Magic, is a synthetic amphetamine and until 2010 it was legal in the UK. It changed my life. Before I tried MCAT I had been teetering at the top of a slope, my behaviour excessive, but not quite worrying. MCAT kicked me hard in the back, and sent me flying down that slope at rapid speed.

I knew that the drug was making its way round the circle of friends I spent time in the pub with, and it sparked my interest. I'd heard the high from it was amazing, and that it was incredibly cheap compared to cocaine.

'Do you know anyone selling that MCAT stuff?' I asked a friend who was in the know one night.

'I do, Matty,' he said, scribbling down a number. 'Just give this guy Carlos a call.'

I bought £10 worth, meeting Carlos on Princess Elizabeth Way. And that was it. I was off. A new habit was born, and it carried me away.

My friend Sean and I split the £10 that night and made the MCAT last until the morning, spinning with the high of it. We gurned, grinding our teeth and laughing at the world until almost 8am, our pupils like pinpricks in the early morning light.

Sean's brother came to pick Sean up to take him to work that morning. He took one look at him and shook his head in disbelief.

'You can't come into work like that!' he told Sean, then turned to me, sniggering in amusement.

'I've got work in...' I checked my watch, 'about an hour!' Sean's brother just laughed.

The comedown was hideous; anxiety and paranoia like I'd never experienced, but the high was just as amazing as I'd been promised. I started taking it as much as I could, using more and more as my tolerance grew. I soon learned that I could avoid the comedown by just carrying on the party, and my usage increased.

Within a few short weeks I had begun doing lines at work just to keep me going, cutting them on the staff toilet, and snorting them before going back on the tills. White powder was often clinging to my nostrils as I served customers, and I was jittery and anxious if I didn't get my hit.

As my drug use increased, my health declined, and it plunged downwards with incredible speed. I was snorting so much that my nose was bloody and raw, and I had frequent dripping nosebleeds. I would go down for a line, and come back up with my nostrils screaming at me, smears of blood on the note I'd used.

I'd also pretty much stopped eating and sleeping. My weight plummeted, and my mental health was delicately clinging on. I felt agitated and anxious at the slightest thing, and I was permanently on edge and slightly angry. I also felt ill almost all the time, although I could mask this with more and more drugs.

One night, I ended up in a flat of someone who I saw regularly round the pub. There were four of us crammed into a small and grubby living room, and I was dishing out MCAT to everyone who wanted it. One of the men we were with had a gas canister used to refill lighters. He kept inhaling the fumes, and I remember thinking that he was going to drop dead any second; it was truly terrifying behaviour, even for someone as heavily into drugs as I was.

I began to cut up some more lines on a broken mirror. Each time anyone wanted a line, I'd carry the mirror over to them and hold it up to their nose as they snorted. It took a long time for me to realise that the jagged edges of the mirror were digging into my hands, and I had blood running down my wrists. As long as it didn't get mixed with the drugs, I didn't care. I was so off my head that I couldn't feel it at all.

Towards the end of the night, I lined up the last of my drugs on the mirror and prepared to do a line. This was the exact moment when one of the blokes we were with stood up to go to the toilet and knocked the mirror. All the MCAT dissolved into the filthy carpet and I panicked. It was early in the morning by now, and there were no dealers who would answer the phone at this time. I got down on my knees and began to snort the stuff directly from the floor, choking and gagging on the dust that came up through my nose. It was disgusting, but I needed the drugs.

I began to do more and more as my tolerance grew, and I also began to use MDMA, another party drug. I did this to excess as well; I could usually get a few lines out of a gram, but one night, three of us split two grams. We poured it all out onto a wheelie bin in an alleyway, and chopped it into three fat lines, each of us snorting an entire third each. MDMA is much more usually swallowed; snorting it feels a bit like snorting crushed glass, but it gives you a more intense high, and so of course, that's what we did. That night was completely wild. We went clubbing, and I literally felt like my entire body was vibrating. My eyes were huge, and it felt like I could feel my eyeballs shaking. My entire face felt warm and I was unable to blink.

'Fuck me, Matt,' said a friend when she saw me in the smoking area, 'what have you taken?'

All I could do was grin manically.

Despite the fun times and the highs, things got scary very quickly. One day I came in from work, bone weary and out of drugs. I headed up to my room and lay down on my bed, desperate for some sleep before I hit the town again that night.

Suddenly I couldn't move. I was frozen, stuck, quivering, my eyes open, but unable to speak or even shout. There was a glass of water perched on my bedside table, and I tried to move towards it, to knock it off and alert my parents to what was going on. I couldn't. All my muscles were spasming and I was completely trapped in my own body. I genuinely thought I was about to die.

It seemed like at least five minutes I was stuck there, spasming alone on my bed, but really it could have been only a minute at most. I slowly regained control of my muscles and lay there panting. *Fuck*, I thought, *that was scary*.

I never told anyone. Not even when it happened again a few weeks later. By the time it happened for the third time I was less frightened. I chalked it down to an unavoidable side effect of the drugs, and, convinced by now that I wasn't going to die, carried on like I had done before. I was dancing with death on a daily basis, but quitting the MCAT wasn't something I was prepared to do.

***

My MCAT habit put even more pressure on my already precarious financial situation, and, in utter desperation, I began stealing from the shop. This was a new low for me. I have always been an honest person, and stealing was never something that had crossed my mind before. But I was desperate, withdrawing from the drugs, and the only way I could keep funding my habit was to add to my income. I justified it to myself by saying that I had no choice. I also told myself it was fine because it was a company, and not a person. This attitude allowed me to dodge the guilt, or at least put it to the back of my mind.

The stealing began with cigarettes, which were kept in a locked cage in the stockroom. The keys to this had to be signed in and out from a safe within the manager's office, and so getting them was a stressful event in itself.

I'd have to wait for someone to ring the manager bell on the shop floor. When I heard Sally's heels clicking across the shop, I'd leg it, running to the office. I'd rapidly open the safe, grab the keys to the cigarette cage, get the fags out, and then run back, re-locking and replacing everything as I went. I moved as fast as I could, and I was often out of breath by the time I'd completed my mission. I'd lean against the wall, heart pounding, sweating from the exertion, but feeling relief that I'd be able to afford drugs that night.

This was a system that worked, and I got away with it for a very long time. I'd smuggle the cigarettes out of the shop by cramming them down the front of my trousers and walking out.

'See ya!' I'd say as I left, cheerfully waving goodbye to everyone. I'd often have hundreds of pounds of stolen stock on me as I left, and yet for a long time no-one was any the wiser.

I nearly got caught once early on. I was in the cigarette cage, grabbing armfuls of whatever I could, when Sally appeared in the door of the warehouse. I stopped dead, staring at her, the cigarettes clattering out of my arms and onto the floor in pure shock. My mouth was so dry I couldn't find any words. I'd been caught.

It was only when I managed to focus on Sally's face that I realised all was not lost. She was looking at me in amusement.

'Ha,' she snorted, 'butterfingers!' My heart was beating so fast I was sure she could hear it, but she went about her day, the incident forgotten. It was a very close call, but it wasn't enough to stop me.

I sold the stolen goods in the pub, which was right next door to the shop. It is really amazing that I went on for so long without getting caught; I was open about my stealing, and conspicuous in my selling.

'Got these from work!' I'd shout to anyone who looked like they'd buy something off me, 'half price fags!'

It wasn't long before I was stealing anything I could get my hands on. Literally anything that was worth selling would end up shoved down my trousers, or in my pockets. I also began swiping cash, taking handfuls of £20 notes every time I was working on the tills. I got sneaky with avoiding the cameras that I knew were everywhere, pretending to scan things, and perfecting my slight of hand. I was a magician in my own way, and a successful one at that.

***

My life got slowly more and more chaotic. It was a blurry time for me, a messy crash of drink and drugs and poor behaviour. I craved excitement and the buzz I got from drugs, and the stealing and drinking fed into this. I was spinning out of control, but I couldn't see it; I was convinced that I was having fun.

I began to take my mum's car at night for another thrill, speeding down the back country roads in a haze. Mum had absolutely no idea that I was doing this; I'd sneak downstairs and grab the keys off the hook by the door, returning them in the early hours of the morning.

This behaviour was reckless beyond belief. I was always, without exception, either incredibly drunk or incredibly high, and, to add to the insanity, I had no idea how to turn the headlights on. I'd whizz round in the middle of the night in complete darkness, just for the rush of it. I'd be mere inches from hedges, and well over the speed limit, rattling round corners as fast as I could take them. The fact I didn't injure or kill myself, or anyone else, is something I never let myself forget.

One night, I finally got pulled over by the police. I was high out of my brains, with a huge amount of MCAT still on me. I

51

saw the blue lights flashing over the dashboard, and, thinking surprisingly quickly, shoved the bag full of white powder into my sock.

'What are you doing mate?' the policeman asked me, tapping on my window. He was quite visibly gobsmacked at the lack of headlights, although luckily for me, my driving had been absolutely perfect.

'Yeah,' I said, concentrating hard on seeming sober, 'this is a new car, and I don't know how to turn the headlights on.' The policeman looked at me for a moment, then reached through the window and twisted the indicator. Light flooded the road and lit up my face, which looked sheepish, and undeniably unfocused.

'I'm going to have to breathalyse you, mate,' said the policeman, catching the unmistakable whiff of alcohol that clung to me, and taking in the very weird situation. I was under the legal limit. However, it quickly became apparent that I was in a stolen car, and I was taken down to the police station.

I was searched when we got there, as is standard. I had absolutely no intention of giving up my drugs, and so I didn't declare them, hoping for the best. It paid off. The policeman searching me ran his hands over my arms and legs, and then down to my ankles. He missed the MCAT and the plastic card that was stashed away, and, unable to believe my luck, I found myself locked in the cell with it.

My luck continued. How I wasn't seen on the cameras snorting lines I don't know. I spent all night in the cell, and then all morning, and I was finally picked up just after lunchtime the next day. I'd spent the entire night snorting the remainder of my MCAT, and I was flying. I got into Mum's car feeling incredible; I didn't care what I'd done, and I wasn't even sorry. I was just happy I'd got away with it.

And get away with it I did. Mum decided not to press charges, so I was never charged for taking the car. Instead, I got a fine and a few points on my licence for driving without insurance. I didn't even own a car at the time, so this didn't bother me. I swanned out of court feeling on top of the world, and utterly untouchable.

***

Things couldn't carry on the way they were going, despite my confidence, and everything eventually imploded on me at work. Staff had begun to notice that huge amounts of cigarettes were going missing, and we were closely watched. Then someone in the pub reported to the shop that I was selling stolen goods, and things clicked into place for Sally. That was the beginning of the end, and she set out to catch me.

Despite knowing that it was me who was stealing, actually proving it took Sally a long time – I'd grown good at the stealing by then. I would take the fags and then hide them in the cloakroom, shoving them in empty boxes, and keeping them there until I could sneak them out. As a result, my locker searches revealed nothing, and therefore nothing could be proven. Still, the atmosphere at work was frosty, and I drowned my increasing anxiety in even more drugs and booze, clinging onto anything that made me feel normal.

One day, it finally happened. I'd ramped up my operation, knowing I was likely to be caught, and my friend Kev was working for me by then. His job was to take the goods I stole and get them out of the shop for me. This helped me to avoid the random searches that were getting ever more frequent, and also allowed me to steal even more stock.

I'd given Kev six full bottles of whiskey that morning, pretending to scan them and then handing them over. No-one had said anything, so I assumed we were safe for that day. I told Kev to come back later for his payment; a 12.5g pouch of tobacco.

'There you go, pal,' I said cheerfully when he returned a few hours later. I pretended to wave it over the scanner, as I always did.

'Thanks, Matt,' he said, wandering out the door, 'I'll see you in a bit.'

I stepped back from the till and opened my newspaper, satisfied with a job well done. The door from the warehouse opened, and my colleague, Jess, approached the tills.

'Hiya Matt, I've been told to take over from you. Sally wants to see you in her office.' Her voice gave nothing away, but I still felt a little flash of fear. I shut the newspaper and made my way to the back of the shop. I knew it was only a matter of time – could this be it?

It was. I walked into the office and saw myself on CCTV, the tape paused at the exact moment I'd been pretending to scan the tobacco for Kev. Sally was looking at me, caught between relief and disapproval, another manager sat next to her. I'd been caught. Really caught, this time.

'What's going on here, Matt?' said Sally, waving at the screen.

'I… I don't know, Sal?' I said, trying to lie to her, even with stone cold evidence in front of us. 'I was just serving a customer.'

'You weren't though, Matt, were you?' she said, 'you were stealing from us, as you've been doing for months now.' My number was up, and I knew it. I nodded, unsure of what else to do.

'If I resign, what will happen? Like, will you report this to the police?' I was too tired to lie anymore.

'I really don't know, Matt,' said Sally tiredly. She rubbed her temples in exhaustion, closing her eyes. 'I'll ask my district manager and find out for you. For now, I need you to leave. Your contract has been terminated, effective immediately, and I'm going to have to ask you to get out of the shop.'

I left through the back door, reeling in the shock of it. I had known it was coming, of course I had, but I'd been trying not to think about it. The fact that it was all over was overwhelming.

I went straight to the pub. I couldn't think what else to do, but I knew I needed something to get me away from my racing thoughts. I downed a pint, and then another and then another. At some point I got a call from Sally.

'Matt,' she said, 'I've spoken to my manager, and as long as you resign, we won't take this to the police.' The relief was incredible. I'd stolen thousands of pounds worth of stock over the last year or so, and prison was a very real possibility that had been bouncing round my head. I'd got away with it – again!

High on alcohol and freedom, I told my parents, Dutch courage masking my real feelings. They were disappointed, worried for me, and, above all, not surprised. It was obvious that

I was heading for some sort of crash, and had been for months. I think they were just pleased things hadn't turned out worse.

I look back on this time now, and, strange as it sounds, I feel overwhelmingly grateful. Being caught stealing, and therefore being forced to resign, although horrendous at the time, was ultimately a good thing. I'd been earning so much money that my supply of drugs was almost limitless. As my tolerance grew, my usage did as well, as I was spiralling fast. To this day, I truly believe that if I hadn't got caught, I would have been on my way to an early death.

I was, and still am, lucky in so many ways. All of this behaviour - the stealing; the drug driving; the incredibly high drug use – could have ended with me dead or in prison. It could also potentially have got me help much earlier, but I like to take positives from life when I can. Through the luck of the Irish blood that runs through my veins, I emerged from the wreckage of my time in the shop basically unscathed.

Chapter Six

For six weeks after I left my job, I did nothing but drink. It was an awful time, depressing and hopeless, and my anxiety was so high that I truly didn't know what else to do.

Life was not going well for Deb either; Phil had left her a couple of weeks after I'd been sacked, and we never found out why. Whatever the reason, Deb joined me in my pit of despair, quitting her job out of grief and stress, and maybe a bit of solidarity. The two of us sat in Deb's house drowning our sorrows for weeks on end, joined on occasion by Harry. I was hopelessly poor, so drugs were out of the question, and I never used around Deb anyway; she hated drugs. Instead, we scraped together what little cash we could and bought cans of Strongbow and boxes of cheap supermarket wine.

I grew even closer to Deb during this time, the two of us pulling together in our mutual despair. Deb sold most of her stuff, and we ended up sat on camping furniture as we drank.

'Fuck it babe,' she'd say as someone picked up her sofa, 'it don't matter.' We'd sit on our folding chairs at the end of the night, pooling our final few coins for one last tin of beer.

I carried on stealing. I'd been banned from the shop of course, but I began pocketing stuff from the corner shop close to Deb's and selling it on cheap. On days when I was desperate, I'd just head straight for the cider and swipe that, filling the pockets of my Barbour coat with tins and clanking straight out the door.

Everyone in the local area knew that I was a thief and a loser by then. I would walk round the estate with my hood up, avoiding eye contact with everyone. The local little old ladies would glare at me as I passed, knowing who I was, and I'd cower away from them in shame.

I began this period of unemployment with a rule that I wouldn't start drinking until midday. This seemed acceptable to me, and meant I could keep convincing myself that I didn't have a problem. As the weeks dragged on, however, I began pushing this; and the drinking began to start earlier and earlier in the day.

I was soon hammering the booze almost as soon as I woke up. I'd roll out of bed and start swigging on cider as I walked to Deb's, and I'd begin drinking whatever we could afford as soon as I got there.

Despite this increase in boozing, I actually got much healthier during this time. Before I was caught stealing from the shop, I'd been near enough on death's door, so skinny that my bones were protruding under my skin. I was all angles and big eyes, a complete physical wreck. Once I quit the drugs, the weight piled on. This was mainly because I was finally eating again. I wasn't eating well, but at least I was getting something down me. Harry cooked quite a lot when he was around, and when he wasn't, we'd scavenge, ramming down whatever we could steal, or whatever was in the cupboard. I became quite partial to spaghetti hoops, eaten cold straight from the tin. The increased diet, vile as it was at times, worked wonders, and I began to feel healthier again very quickly.

***

Tensions were understandably sky high at home. My parents were frantic; desperate for me to find another job, caught between irritation and concern at the situation I'd created for myself.

'You have to do something, Matt!' my dad said to me, Mum nodding her head next to him.

'Please, Matt?' she said, 'sign on the dole or get a job – anything! You can't keep moping around here for free.'

'I can't,' is all I'd say. 'I can't do anything.' It sounds like an excuse, like I just couldn't be bothered, but it was so much more than that. Years of drugging and drinking had hit my mental health hard, and I was battling with overwhelming anxiety daily. The thought of walking into town and going through a job centre appointment filled me with such an unbearable fear that I was incapable of doing it. Instead, I just carried on the way I was, drinking and drinking and drinking.

In October, six weeks after I'd lost my job, I got a call from Lee Sykes. Lee is a close family friend, and he owns a plastic manufacturing factory in Gloucester. He'd clearly heard about my situation from my parents.

'Hi Matt,' he said down the phone, 'I hear you're out of work. Do you want a job?'

'I do…' I said warily. I wasn't sure I could handle the pressure of an interview and an application process.

'All you have to do is come up to Gloucester and meet the man who runs the place. The job's basically yours,' he said, and I jumped at it. It was the perfect solution.

The next day I was shown round Lee's factory by Ray, the boss and for the first time in months I felt something like excitement blooming in my gut. I knew nothing about plastic manufacturing or about what was going on around me, but the job seemed interesting, and definitely a step up from the shop. It was a set Monday to Friday structure, and the thought of not working weekends was enticing. I was sold.

That evening I was sat on the bus, rumbling my way home to Cheltenham, when I got a call.

'Hiya Matt, it's Ray from the factory.'

'Hi, how's it going?' I said, knowing that he was calling with good news.

'Good mate,' he said, 'it was great to meet you today, and I'm calling to offer you a job. When would you be available to start?' I was elated. I couldn't wait to get going.

'Is tomorrow too early?' I said jokingly. Unfortunately for me, Ray didn't take it as a joke.

'Yeah, cool mate,' he said, 'I'll see you tomorrow at 8am. Bye!' I put the phone down in shock. I had a job, and I started tomorrow.

***

I arrived at the factory the next day, on time, and keen to get going. The first day was brilliant; I felt immediately settled and happy. *This is it, Matt*, I told myself, *this is a fresh start*. I collected my uniform and looked around me in wonder. It was an exciting time, and I thought I'd be there forever.

And for a while, it really did seem like I'd managed to turn myself around. I bought myself a car and happily whizzed between Gloucester and Cheltenham, working hard, and staying off the drugs. I was still drinking, but only at weekends, and it never affected my work. My mental health stabilised, and I began to feel almost happy again, memories of the crazy few months before all but gone from my memory.

I'd been at the factory for a few months when I decided to pick up the MCAT again. I don't know why. Nothing happened, nothing triggered it, but I bought a gram on a night out, buzzing with the thrill of feeling good again. I cut up a line on the toilet in the pub and then stood there staring at it, unable to decide whether to do it or not. Even then, on some level, I knew it was a bad idea. MCAT had turned my life upside down just a few months ago. I had hated the paranoia, the anxiety, the nosebleeds, the seizures, the weight loss, the lack of money. But then again, the high was amazing for a short while.

I leaned down and sniffed the entire line up through my nose.

The decline after this was, once again, rapid. The weight dropped off me, and within a few short weeks I had become obsessed again. I began to take any drug I could get my hands on, regularly snorting cocaine and MDMA as well as MCAT, just happy with any substance that made me feel less like myself.

Work began to suffer as well, and my ambition and excitement over my new job dropped rapidly.

'Come and learn how to operate this machine,' Ray would say to me, beckoning me over. I'd just shake my head. It seemed like far too much effort to learn anything new, and I didn't care anymore. All my energy was focused on getting through work, and out into the weekend. The world of drugs was, once again, pulling me down into a hole, and my life orbited around it once more.

Slowly, the weekday night partying starting creeping in. My previous 'weekends only' rule suddenly didn't seem to matter anymore, and work didn't really help. There was a big drinking culture in the factory – there were guys who were raging alcoholics, who would come in with the shakes every day, stinking of booze. It was all good fun coming into work in a state, and we'd take the piss out of each other on a regular basis. Being a bit of a mess was seen as amusing and I justified it in my head as all being good fun. *Everyone else is doing it*, I'd think, *why shouldn't I?*

***

I was out in a nightclub one night that summer, high on whatever powder I'd managed to get my hands on that evening, and dancing like a maniac, when I saw a girl. The drugs had made me uninhibited, and I was very much in the market for a one-night stand. I approached her with an unearned confidence, dancing around her until she noticed me.

'Have you taken something?' she yelled over the pounding music.

'No!' I screamed back, a blatant lie. I don't really know why I lied, except that something inside me told me to; I guess I wanted to impress her. It worked.

Her name was Lucy, and the attraction was mutual. We didn't sleep together that night, but something drew me to her, and we met up again shortly afterwards. That was when I realised that I really liked her. It wasn't just about sex; I really liked her as a person. She made me feel very safe and loved, and she was kind and thoughtful.

That sense of wanting to be loved and looked after had kicked in again, and I became besotted with her very quickly. We began seeing each other not long after first meeting, and naturally fell into a relationship. She, correctly, suspected that I'd been on drugs the night we met. Even so, she gave me a second chance.

'You can't be taking drugs if you want to be with me, Matt,' she said, 'I just can't have that in my life.' I'd fallen head over heels, and I'd have done anything for her by then. That included stopping using and so that's what I did.

Again, I believe this saved my life. I'd reached that breaking point again, where my body was beginning to give up, and my head was screaming for some time off. I was still drinking, and still partying, but the drugging stopped, and, as before, my health crept back.

The relationship with Lucy was good, and I was very happy, caught in the whirlwind of new love. Deb was happy for me as well, and my mental health reached a good and steady place. Deb was seeing someone new by then, a man called Dale who worked with me. I'd introduced the two of them, and they were also blissfully happy. The four of us would often hang out together, drinking and talking, and life seemed good once again; like everything was rumbling along the right track.

Even my parents noticed the change.

'You seem to be doing really well, Matt,' my mum said one day, as I headed out to work.

'I am,' I said, smiling at her. And I meant it.

And then everything came crashing down.

Firstly, just two weeks before Christmas, Lucy dumped me. She sent me a text telling me that it was over. I hadn't seen it coming, and I was utterly devastated. I begged her for a week to get back with me, on some level convinced that it might happen. I'd text her and call her, desperately trying to persuade her to give it another go. This misguided hope kept me off the drugs for another week, and I drank myself into oblivion instead, wallowing in my loneliness.

After a week of begging in vain, I realised that Lucy genuinely wasn't coming back. The feeling of heartbreak and rejection hit me like a train, and I realised that there was nothing stopping me from using drugs anymore. I also realised that drugs would help me escape these feelings – and if there was ever a time I needed to escape, it was now.

I bought a gram of MCAT and took it to the pub again, looking at it on the toilet, a mirror of how I'd been a few months earlier. *This is going to blow my head off,* I thought, *is this really a good idea?* I knew that it would be the start of a dangerous road; I'd been using MCAT for long enough to know what the future would look like if I developed a habit again. Twice now I'd tumbled down that road, and twice now I had just about clawed myself back. I knew what my life would turn into.

And then I remembered Lucy, remembered that she wasn't coming back, and remembered that I had Christmas looming ahead of me, and I had to be cheerful and happy for my family. Crucially, I remembered that amazing, blissful high. *Fuck it,* I thought.

I felt different after I did the line. It was better than drink, better than moping by myself in my bedroom. With just one line, the world felt okay again, and I felt happy and peaceful. My problems dissolved and floated away, and I found myself able to

61

face life again. *Right,* I thought, *this is clearly the way forward. I'll just start doing this again.*

That was the worst Christmas ever. For the first time the feelings I had while I was sober were utterly unbearable, and I had to use drink and drugs to cope. I moped around the house, stressed and rattling when I couldn't get my hands on any drugs, completely dazed and out of it when I had something in my system.

My parents had no idea about the drugs, but they could tell that I was both deeply unhappy and drinking excessively. Dad came into my room several times that Christmas to check on me, sitting on the end of my bed to chat.

'Is everything okay, son?' he'd say awkwardly, clearly wanting to help, but not knowing how.

'I'm fine, Dad,' I'd reply. My problems felt so huge that I had no idea where to start. He'd nod and leave the room quietly, and I'd be left alone again. That was fine by me. I didn't feel like I could talk to anyone. Drugs and drink were my only friends, and that was all I wanted.

The second thing that went wrong was that Deb and I fell out in a huge, catastrophic argument. She and Dale were both drinking huge amounts. Deb had always been a big drinker, but she was steadily drinking more and more, with Dale doing the same alongside her. Their relationship revolved around alcohol, and I could see the difference in her behaviour. I could tell that her partying wasn't doing her any good.

One night I went out with her and her family, and her mum also noticed the change in her. She pulled me to one side to talk to me, worried.

'Is Deb drinking too much, Matt?' she asked me. She was so scared, her voice full of concern for her daughter, that I didn't have the heart to lie to her.

'I think so,' I replied. I genuinely did this out of care for Deb; if she needed help, I wanted her to get it. Deb, when she found out, didn't see it like that. We had a screaming row, with her accusing me of meddling, of getting involved in her personal life when I didn't understand anything. She yelled at me over and over, saying that I was attempting to ruin her relationship just because I was heartbroken. It was huge, and dramatic, and we didn't speak for a long time after that.

Deb had been such an important person in my life, and I felt her absence like grief. Life just wasn't the same without her in it, and I felt incredibly lost and lonely. We did speak again, years later, but our friendship was never the same. It was a swift transition from being best friends to mere acquaintances and it was extremely painful.

Deb also hated drugs, and had made that very clear, and so my friendship with her had kept me from constantly using. Once she was out of my life, I felt like a balloon cut free; I floated away, with nothing to keep me grounded. My drug use increased even more; I was now an everyday user, and totally uncomfortable being sober.

Incredibly, I was still holding down my job at this point, although my mental state had become a point of concern. I'd regularly turn up hammered or high, sometimes in such a state that I'd get sent home.

'We can't have you at work like this, Matt,' Ray would say kindly, and I'd stumble back to my car and drive drunkenly home, pouring myself back into bed with relief.

The fact I had a problem was becoming obvious to people around me, although no one knew the extent. I was still managing to hide my drug use from my parents, and they were comforted by the fact that 'at least I wasn't on drugs'. Even so, my behaviour was worrying, and my mental health was teetering along with it.

***

I met my friend Stuart through Deb that summer, and I'd begun hanging around with him a lot. We'd stayed good friends even after Deb and I fell out, and I was grateful for his friendship in my messed-up state. He was a magician, a real character, and excellent company. He was also very protective of me. It was obvious to him that I was severely unwell by this point, but he knew better than to stop me. Instead, he gave me safe place to use, and we spent many hours together in his flat. He rarely used drugs and only drank occasionally, but he'd sit with me while I slowly got wrecked, just listening to me and providing support.

One night I ran out of coke, and I went to pick up some more. I was off my head, and I can't remember why Stuart didn't stop me from driving, but he didn't. I left his flat, got in my car, and drove haphazardly to an area called Whaddon to meet a dealer. I didn't care that I shouldn't have been driving – all I was focused on was getting more drugs.

As I pulled up in Whaddon, I managed to slam my front wheel against the kerb, sending the hubcap rolling off with the impact. My mind was so focused on scoring that I didn't even care. I abandoned my car at an odd angle in the road, and jumped straight into the dealer's car, handing over my money and grabbing my drugs as quickly as I could. Cocaine was the aim, and I just wanted to get back to Stuart's to carry on the sesh.

I was driving back through a housing estate called Elmfield when I saw blue flashing lights in my rear-view mirror. To this day I have no idea whether they were real or not. I suspect that I had simply taken so many drugs that I was paranoid and hallucinating. Real or not, I was petrified, and I slammed on the accelerator in an attempt to outrun them. I drove at high speed, staring in my mirror rather than at the road, terrified I was going to see a police car at any moment.

I glanced back at the road briefly, and to my horror saw that I was heading straight for a fence.

Panic set in and I swerved the steering wheel without thinking. This sent the car skidding uncontrollably across the road, wheels screeching, and the whole car spinning around me. It finally came to a stop, smashing against a lamppost, smoke seeping out of the engine. I'd hit my head with the impact, and I sat up, blinking and coughing, assessing myself for any more damage. I'd been blessed by luck again, and apart from a bang on the head, I was unharmed. *Wow*, I thought, *I'd better get these drugs back before the police catch me.*

And so that's exactly what I did. I managed to get the car back to Stuart's, and I just carried on using. The car was a write-off; I'd managed to bend the axle beyond repair. I didn't care. My entire focus in life was about drugs, and as long as I had them, I didn't care about the rest of the wreckage burning around me.

Although Stuart hadn't stopped me from driving that night, my car crash was a turning point for him, and his attitude towards my drug use. He sat me down one day for a serious talk.

'Matt, I think we need to get you some help,' he said, looking at me kindly.

'Nah, I'm fine Stuart, I really am,' I said. The concept of telling anyone about what was going on seemed horrendous, and I couldn't face it.

'Why don't we start small? Do you think you could tell your mum?' I was horrified. My parents had no idea that I was doing drugs, and I knew that they'd be heartbroken.

'I can't do it,' I said, shaking my head.

'You can,' said Stuart kindly, and I felt a flash of something close to hope. Maybe it wasn't too late to get out of this mess. I knew that the first step would be to tell someone.

'Alright,' I said, 'but can we do it here? Can she come to your flat?' Stuart agreed to that, and so I told her shortly afterwards, with Stuart standing by for moral support.

Mum was, as predicted, horrified. She cried, scared for me, and saddened that she'd not noticed. She was also hopeful, and proud that I'd been honest with her.

'We'll get you some help, Matt,' she said, hugging me. Stuart reassured her as well.

'There's so much you can do,' he told her, 'we'll help him get the help he needs.'

I contacted a charity called Turning Point after that conversation, promising Mum that I could get some help, and that I could sort out my own mess. I didn't want her to get involved. I was self-aware enough to realise that all this was my problem, and that I couldn't put the burden of it onto anyone else.

It took a lot for me to make that first phone call. I had several drinks and a considerable amount of MDMA before I could even bring myself to pick up the phone. But I had promised my mum, and so I did, my hands and voice shaking. I remember talking to the lady on the phone at Turning Point trying desperately to keep my jaw from swinging wildly, feeling on the brink of madness.

It's worth noting here that Turning Point is an amazing charity, and they help so many people. They offer everything from detox to supported housing, as well as community support and drug and alcohol education. I was offered counselling, and appointments with a support worker, and I began going regularly.

Unfortunately, the nature of addiction means that it is impossible to get better if you don't want to. And I had absolutely no desire to stop using. My thoughts were too painful, and my drinking and using was a vital crutch that helped me stay sane. I went to the sessions that were given to me and lied through my teeth about my behaviour. I was so miserable and anxious by this point that I often had to drink a considerable amount before I even went in.

My parents had no experience of addiction, and so I found it was easy to pull the wool over their eyes.

'Yeah, it's really helpful,' I'd say, wobbling in from counselling, stinking of booze.

'Have you been drinking?' Mum would ask, concerned.

'Yeah, yeah, they tell us that the odd drink is fine' I said, 'I'm not using anything anymore.'

To my parents, and the friends I had left, Turning Point seemed to be living up to its name. I was getting help, and seemed, if not fixed, at least a bit better. Inside, I knew full well that nothing was getting better. I couldn't stop using drugs, I couldn't stop drinking, and I didn't want to. Everything around me was crumbling, and life felt impossible.

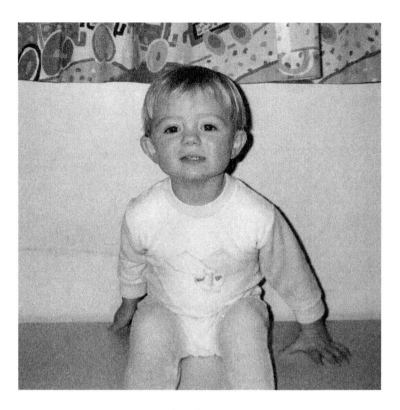

Aged two.

In my penultimate year of Swindon Village Primary School.

With some friends aged around 14 or 15.

The subway where I was arrested for possession of cannabis.

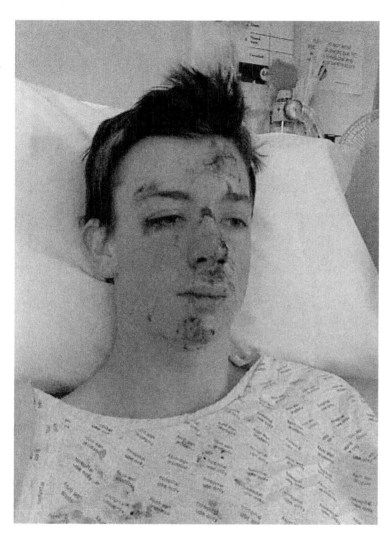

Following getting hit by a car at 60mph, my face after being stitched up on 30th March 2008.

The car that hit me was a write-off.

Drowning my sorrows in my local pub in 2016. This was a particularly dark time for me.

Extravagant spending. After receiving my inheritance I found it very difficult to walk past a jeweller's without going in and buying something.

A still image of a video showing me getting arrested by armed police in November 2018.

The building where I lived up until rehab.

Out with friends and family not long before rehab. I became an expert in hiding what was really going on in my life and even though I was visibly deteriorating, nobody knew the true extent of my problems.

This picture was taken while I was being checked into rehab on
18th July 2019.

Oasis Runcorn. Top: the outside of the building. Bottom left: the smoking area. Bottom right: the room I stayed in while I was there.

Clean and sober. Helping my dad at his allotment. This was at the peak of my weight gain before I started to get fit and healthy.

Happy and healthy after completing an early morning run.
Recovery is amazing!

Chapter Seven

I'd been working with Turning Point for a while when Stuart rang me. Ironically, this was a turning point for me, but in a very different way.

'Hiya Matt, I'm going away for two weeks,' he said, 'if you fancy a break from living with your folks, you can stay at mine and look after the dog.'

Obviously I said yes. I was more than happy to help out, but for all the wrong reasons. I knew that I was going downhill, and fast. I also knew that I had no desire to stop taking drugs, despite what I was telling everyone around me. I didn't care about the dog. Living in Stuart's flat would just be a perfect opportunity to get really messed up without having to hide it from anyone.

Elated by the thought of uninterrupted freedom, I booked two weeks off work. I maxed out all the payday loans I could and bought enough coke and booze to keep me going for the whole time I was there. I headed out to meet dealers when I needed some more, and spent the rest of the time sat in semi-darkness, the hours trickling by as I used and drank and drank and used. It was a miserable time, but I felt the closest to safe I had in a while. My own company was all I wanted, and not having to answer concerned questions from my parents felt like a breath of fresh air.

Even I had my limits, however, and one night I got bored of Stuart's flat. He lived in a horrible rough block of flats, and there was nothing to do. There was nothing to even look at out the window, just skinny pigeons and soggy litter. I felt itchy and restless, driven slightly mad by the four walls that surrounded me. Swallowing several gulps of whiskey to settle my nerves, I got behind the wheel of my car and headed for the pub, utterly sick of being alone.

I was in luck; there were plenty of people in the pub who knew me and were happy to spend a few hours with me talking about nothing. I sunk a few pints, feeling that familiar warmth spread through me. I felt bolstered by the company and the conversation after so long on my own. I sat down with a loose acquaintance, Marcus, and began talking to him about my drug use.

I was showing off, boasting about the amounts I got through, and the ways I avoided questioning. Suddenly an idea struck me, and I looked Marcus in the eye.

'Yeah, I'd love to try crack you know,' I said. I truly don't know why I said this. I think I'd just reached a point where I needed something stronger to reach the same highs. Or perhaps, in its own way, it was an act of self-harm, or a cry for help. Either way, Marcus's eyes lit up and I knew I'd made the first step down a one-way road.

'Really? I know a bloke,' he said. He drained the remainder of his pint and stood up eagerly. 'Are you okay to drive?'

It was late by then, and I had drunk a lot. I wasn't anywhere near okay to drive, but I did anyway. I squinted at the road as we headed into the slightly seedier areas of Cheltenham, my heart pounding. I couldn't quite believe that I was headed to buy crack. I knew it was a bad idea. I knew I'd get hooked. I knew my life would get even worse than it was already. Still, I kept driving, the pull of a better high too strong to ignore.

'Just here,' said Marcus, after a few minutes of driving, and I parked up at the side of the road. We were in a grim residential area, the houses dilapidated and sad, with broken gates and boarded up windows. Weeds grew everywhere and litter clogged up the gutters, undoubtedly attracting rats and other vermin. I felt nervous. This was unlike any other time I'd picked up drugs. The mess and the filth seemed to illustrate to me that I was entering a different world, but it was nowhere near enough to put me off.

Marcus got out of the car and glanced up and down the street. Satisfied he wasn't being watched, he shuffled up to one of the grubby-looking houses and knocked on the window. I watched from the car, too wary about being seen to get out, but too excited to leave. My heart dropped when Marcus came back to the car with nothing.

'It's alright mate,' said Marcus, laughing at the dismay on my face, 'we just need to go to this other address.' I started the car again and we headed out into the night.

We got the crack eventually. Again, I stayed in the car, watching in anticipation as Marcus made the transaction. My palms were sweating, and I kept glancing around me to check that I was still safe from prying eyes.

'Here we go,' Marcus said as he got back in the car, grinning from ear to ear, 'here we fucking go!'

***

We headed back to Stuart's and sat in his dreary kitchen. The only light was from a bare bulb hanging from the ceiling, and I hadn't bothered to clear up the mess I'd slowly been making during my days alone. Empty glass bottles lay all over the place, the table sticky with spilt whiskey and ash. I'd got into the habit of saving my whiskey bottles once I'd finished them, and they were lined up like trophies along the edge of the table, a sad show of what I'd achieved in the past two weeks. Marcus was unfazed. We swept it all onto the floor and looked at the rocks of crack cocaine in the baggy.

'I'm guessing you don't have a pipe?' asked Marcus, and I shook my head.

'No, I've never done this before,' I replied, almost shaking with the anticipation of it.

'No worries,' he said, 'do you have like a can of anything? Coke or a tinny?'

I handed him an empty can of coke, and watched as he fashioned it into a crack pipe. I was amazed. I was reminded of the days when I'd watch Pisshead Pete rack up a line in the stables; the sense of awe was exactly the same. Marcus even guided me through my first hit, as Pisshead Pete had done years ago.

'Just breathe in until I let go of the hole,' he said, holding the pipe up to my lips. And that's exactly what I did, inhaling the smoke into my lungs, and sealing my fate.

That first hit of crack did very little for me. I don't even recall feeling anything particularly out of the ordinary. I sat in Stuart's kitchen with Marcus until he left, and then drank myself to sleep as usual. I woke up the next morning feeling the same as ever; hungover and dirty, with aching lungs from too much smoking.

Perhaps I could have stopped there. I wasn't hooked, and I hadn't even enjoyed it very much. Maybe I could have decided never to touch it again and got on with my life. I'll never know. Instead, still slightly amazed by Marcus's trick with the coke can, I went to a shop and bought a metal pipe. I wanted more.

I remembered a friend, Declan, who had a crack habit. It wasn't something we'd ever acknowledged, but it was a widely known fact; a nugget of gossip that was widely circulated in the local area, and within my social circle. Desperate to get my hands on another hit, I arranged to meet him at his that night.

'You don't smoke crack,' he scoffed, when I produced my pipe. 'You don't even know what it is, Matt.'

'Watch me,' I said, a little part of my desire to be impressive bubbling to the surface. I flicked my lighter and smoked, watching Declan's face as I did so. He grinned at me, acknowledging with glee that I was now a fellow member of this terrible club. I glowed, both from the crack and from the validation from Declan. That was it. There was the hook. I had officially reached the point of no return.

Although essentially the same drug, the difference between coke and crack cocaine is immense. Coke has very little stigma to it; it's widely used, and widely talked about. As a result, it's easy to get, and dealers tend to be as friendly and as above board as it's possible to be. A crack habit, on the other hand, is a dirty little secret. Declan and I met dealers in awful places; miserable crack dens with dirty mattresses lining the floor, the air heavy with smoke and body odour. I felt dirty and ashamed of what I was doing.

Things got a little blurry for a while after that. All my memories of the few weeks that followed are smashed into one haze of bad decisions and self-destruction. Before long, I had got my hands on a crack dealer's number and began buying crack whenever I had the cash, smoking it in my car or in the pub toilets. Each time I woke up after a crack session I'd feel an incredible guilt, and I'd bin my pipe, swearing that I wouldn't go back. The next time I got drunk, however, that desire for crack would come screeching back, and I'd go back to a corner shop and buy another pipe. I must have spent nearly £100 on pipes alone during my first foray into crack, convinced that each time was going to be my last. My paranoia was terrible, and I was constantly on edge, but I couldn't stop. I was completely hooked.

The mentality of crack is different, as well as the people it attracts. It brings out a desperation in the people who use it regularly; a need that overtakes everything else. Crack addicts who are in the depths of a habit will lie, steal and sell everything they own in order to get more, and I learned this very quickly.

I was hanging out with Marcus again the first time I was ripped off, and it was Declan who stole from me. I'd given him money to pick up for me when he scored, and he came back, passed me the bag and swiftly left again.

'He's ripped you off you know,' said Marcus, looking at the crack in my hand, 'he's taken some of that for himself.'

'Nah, he'd never do that,' I said, laughing at the thought. He had. I was much less trusting after that, keeping both my money and my drugs close to my chest.

My own behaviour was changing as well. Although I wasn't stealing from friends or ripping anyone off, I began chasing that crack high, and everything else in my life suffered as a result. I was on and off at work, regularly taking sick leave, and when I did turn up, I took long breaks and left as early as I possibly could. I was a wreck, mentally and physically; my thoughts were an anxious jumble, and I was bone thin and exhausted. At times, I felt like the drugs were the only thing holding me together. I'd often nip to the toilet when I was working, unable to keep my eyes open for a second longer. I'd line the floor with loo roll and curl up with my hood pulled over my eyes. I'd regularly catch a few minutes of sleep in this way; a frantic power nap that allowed me to function for a few more hours.

My entire personality had changed as well; I was now more anxious than I'd ever been, as well as paranoid and wildly short-tempered. One day a co-worker was teasing me about my rapid weight loss and personality change. It was just a gentle ribbing of the sort that regularly went round at work.

'Been on drugs have you, mate?' said my colleague. I don't know whether he was truly joking, or whether there was concern behind his question, but I didn't take it kindly. Something inside me snapped, and I flipped, screaming at him, unable to control my temper. I was completely incapable of calming down. I felt like I'd lost sight of who I was, and what kept me sane. Near tears, and boiling with rage, I stormed out and drove home. I got drunk that night in my bedroom alone. When I turned up to work the next day, stinking of alcohol, and barely able to walk, I was sent straight home.

This experience triggered something in my head, and I realised I needed to make a serious change. I was still getting help from Turning Point, although it was clear to everyone who tried to help me that I was very unwell. The counselling sessions I'd been having stopped, and I didn't miss them. I was drinking and using far too much for them to be useful anyway. At work, Ray had some idea of what was going on, and we had regular meetings. Between Turning Point, Ray, and my own willpower, I somehow managed to cut out the crack.

I saw this as a complete success, and proof that I wasn't an addict. Quitting crack was easy once I'd made the decision to do it, which meant I couldn't possibly be addicted. I avoided thinking about cocaine and alcohol, and the fact that I'd increased my usage of both substances. Crack had been the big, serious one, and the one that mattered. I was fine. I was going to be fine.

***

At the end of 2016 I managed to get a second job, pulling pints behind the bar at a local community centre. It was crazy that I thought that I could do this, but I needed more cash to feed my drug habit. It was a really old-fashioned place, the kind that had once been a thriving hub, and had now run to seed. It still had the same old brass light fittings and dirty green sofas from its heyday, with a handful of regulars who still came to drink warm pints at the weekend. I really enjoyed the work even so. There would be occasional functions on Saturday nights, and I'd work the bar with a friend, getting steadily drunk and sniffing lines of coke in the toilets. The atmosphere reminded me of my shop days, and I flirted with the customers in the same way, dancing as I collected the glasses throughout the night.

I stole from the community centre as well, just like I had at the shop. It started with the odd drink, and moved on to drinks every shift, and then later handfuls of money. The mix of cocaine and alcohol made me aggressive as well; I used to love the buzz of throwing people out when things got too rowdy.

Mainly, however, things at the community centre were quiet, and I could easily slip away every few minutes to sniff coke. Quite often it was just the boss and his daughter, Saskia, propping up the bar of an evening. They were an odd pair, cliquey and aggressive, and I suspected that they were the reason for the lack of customers. The owner had a strange need to be better than everyone else, and one-upped everyone on absolutely everything they said. If you'd been to Tenerife, he'd been to Elevenerife. Any customers were rapidly put off by this strange behaviour, and the evenings were often long and quiet.

Ignoring the red flags that her dad threw up, I grew close to Saskia, and one night, drunk and high, we slept together in her house around the corner. This was the start of a relationship that grew much bigger.

The relationship mirrored the one I had with Lucy in some ways. I fell for Saskia hard and fast, and we quickly entered into an intense partnership. Saskia also kept me stable in some ways; I had no desire to go back to smoking crack when I was with her. The similarities ended there. While Lucy had been good to me, and I'd felt supported and loved in the relationship, Saskia was cruel and manipulative, and my already low self-confidence took a constant battering.

One night at work I went out the back for a cigarette and saw her locked in an embrace with a man I'd never seen before. He had her pressed up against the brick wall, their faces close together in the semi-darkness. My heart dropped, and I felt a wash of cold anxiety in my gut.

'What the fuck?' I said, approaching them. She shoved him away, and followed me back to the bar, whimpering in an attempt to produce some tears.

'It was nothing, Matt,' she said, 'I love you. I really do.' Recounting this now, it is so clear to me that I was being used; that the words 'I love you' were being brandished as an emotional weapon. Back then, I simply saw it as proof that I was loved, and that someone wanted me. That was all my delicate self-esteem needed to forget what I had just seen.

'I love you too,' I said, ignoring all my doubts. I took her hand and we carried on, all forgiven.

A similar thing happened just a few months later, when we were out partying together. Returning from the bar with handfuls of drinks, I saw Saskia dancing with another man. I had a jealous streak, and I was terrified of losing her, and I could see that what was happening wasn't innocent.

'What the fuck are you doing?!' I roared over the pounding music. Saskia and the man just looked at me, vaguely amused, and I lunged up to him, staring him down aggressively. Within seconds, I was being escorted out by a bouncer.

'Please mate,' I said to the bouncer when I was out on the street, 'can you just go and get my girlfriend so we can go home together?' To his credit, he did, disappearing inside for a few minutes, before returning with a wry smile on his face.

'She's busy mate,' he said to me. I ended that night waiting outside her friend's house in the rain, shouting apologies to her as she hid inside. She'd been ignoring me for hours, rejecting my calls as I rang her over and over. Eventually my phone died, and I just sat waiting for her to acknowledge me outside the house I knew she was in.

'I'm so sorry I thought you'd cheat,' I shouted up into the night, 'this is all my fault.'

I found out later that she had actually cheated on me. Not only that, but she'd got everyone around her to accuse me of being out of order. I came away from that night feeling like I was jealous and controlling, determined to make it up to her.

The manipulative behaviour increased the longer we stayed together. She constantly messaged her ex-husband, telling me that she was talking to him, and yet refusing to tell me what he was saying. This drove me to the brink of insanity; I made up wild scenarios in my head about her leaving me for him, and I eventually looked at her phone for reassurance. I didn't get any. There was message after message from her saying that she loved him, and that she wished they'd never split up. It broke my heart, and I confronted her about it, asking whether she really wanted to be with me. That got me dumped for being a paranoid control freak.

We were constantly on and off, with the off periods always blamed on me. She'd offer sex to other men in front of me, and then ban me from certain pubs because of the way I was looking at the female bar staff. I was constantly apologising, and begging her for forgiveness. The one time I broke up with her, she texted me, furious, saying that she dumped me first. We were back together before long.

Saskia's dad, Nigel, continued to be interfering and, frankly, a complete knob.

'It's so annoying having to shave every day,' I whinged one day, a casual comment made mid-conversation.

'You know nothing, Matt,' said Nigel, 'I have to shave twice in the morning, and then a third time in the evening if I'm going out!'

I began to see where Saskia's behaviour originated from; Nigel was a compulsive liar, and would stop at nothing to be admired and to get his way. It was worrying, but it wasn't enough.

In April 2017 I got an umbilical hernia, and had to go into hospital to have it operated on. Saskia broke up with me again the night before my operation, and didn't even bother telling me. I went to text her before I went to sleep and found myself blocked.

What's up with S? I texted a mutual friend. My phone pinged and my stomach dropped.

Leave her alone you bastard, it said. I was blocked on everything. Every social media app. Every possible way I had of contacting her. Once again, however, we were back together within a few days.

The thing about emotionally abusive relationships is that they make you question your own actions. I began to believe Saskia when she told me that everything that she did was my fault. I began to tell myself that I was a cheater, that I looked too closely at other girls, that I didn't treat her right. Whenever she self-harmed and blamed it on me, I took that on board and blamed myself. Whenever she cheated or flirted and told me I was imagining it, I believed that too, and I began to accept that I was a jealous, paranoid madman. I told myself that I was lucky she stayed with me, that I should be grateful that she overlooked everything that was wrong with me. I felt worthless and terrible.

I had a month off work to get better after my hernia operation. I'd been told not to have sex, but I was still desperate to keep Saskia happy. I knew that refusing to have sex would open me up to more abuse, so I gritted my teeth through the pain and slept with her anyway. I'd take Viagra in order to be able to perform sexually, the steady cocaine use hampering my ability to perform. At times, the combination of cocaine and Viagra made my heart beat almost uncontrollably. I could feel it hammering in my chest, and it stressed me out, but I carried on anyway. Not keeping Saskia happy wasn't an option, and neither was stopping taking cocaine.

We did eventually split up for good. I quit the community centre as a result, again getting away with the stealing. Everyone knew I'd had my hand in the till, but also everyone who worked there was doing the same. No-one ever asked me about it. Once again, I'd got away with it, but this time there was no real sense of relief. I was utterly broken.

***

The relationship with Saskia left me in a complete mess, my confidence shattered. The steady abuse had taken a huge toll on me, and I was convinced that I wasn't good enough for anyone. I wallowed in self-hatred. My drug use had been steady all through the relationship, increasing in times of severe stress, or when I felt unbearably awful about myself. It had, however, been stable, and I had stopped myself from losing control. Now, with Saskia a thing of the past, and nothing to keep me trying at life, I increased my using once again.

Throughout this time, I'd continued working at the factory. My lack of crack usage had meant I'd kept up a reasonably good front, and Ray had even commented on how good I'd seemed in our meetings.

'You're doing so well, Matt,' he'd say to me, 'keep it up'.

Then I took two months off for my hernia, and came back single and devastated. I quickly slipped back into old behaviours, falling asleep at work and losing my temper at the smallest thing. I was steering clear of crack, but taking huge amounts of anything else I could get my hands on. I shaved my head while high one night, a true cry for help that didn't go unnoticed. I was given a week off work.

'Please try to sort yourself out, Matt,' said Ray, 'we really care about you here.'

I should have used my week off to get some help. Instead, I saw it as a chance to get drunk and high with nothing to get up for the next day. I was sat in Wetherspoons in Cheltenham one morning that week, high, and nearly delirious, muttering to myself. My nerves were jangling, and I was sipping on a pint to stay calm. Suddenly I saw a man who'd been in the papers a lot recently. He was a convicted rapist, newly released from prison, and, gunning for a fight, I saw red. I charged over, interrupting the conversation he'd been having with a friend.

'YOU FUCKING RAPIST!' I screamed. I smashed into him with my fists, kicking him when he fell to the floor, screaming at him over and over. I used two chairs to swing both feet into his head, then carried on battering him, absolutely caught in the moment, unconcerned with any consequences.

'Stop!' he shouted, desperately trying to defend himself with his arms, 'stop mate!'

'Fucking rapist,' I repeated, continuing anyway. The rest of the pub just stared at me. It was 9am on a weekday, and the place was full of red-faced alcoholic old men trying to have a quiet pint. I only stopped screaming and fighting when the manager grabbed me from behind.

'Out,' she snapped, steering me towards the door.

'But he's a fucking rapist,' I said, my rage bubbling over into hysterical laughter. Out on the street, I pulled my hood up, hiding my shiny bald head from the police I was sure were now after me. I continued wandering the streets, sniggering to myself, my mental health teetering on a knife edge.

That was the beginning of the end, or the end of that period of my life at least. I went back to work, and lasted about a week.

The less money I had, the more I was using alcohol instead of drugs, and I'd reached a stage where I was withdrawing badly when I didn't have booze in my system. I turned up at the factory one morning feeling sick and violently shaking, and suddenly realised I'd had enough. I'd had enough of work, of myself, of everything that my life had become. I put my coat on and headed out the door, unable to think of anything except drinking.

'Matt!' said Ray, 'MATT! Where are you going?'

I turned round at the door and looked at him sadly, leaning against the doorframe to give myself some strength. I'd made my choice, and I knew there was no going back now. I was too messed up to be at work, and I knew it.

'I can't do this anymore, Ray,' I said, 'I just can't do this anymore.'

I walked to my car and drove home, climbing into bed and drinking myself to sleep. It felt like the end, and I knew something had to change. Luckily for me, it was about to. Far from the end, this was the beginning of something bigger. My luck was changing, and my way out lay just round the corner.

Chapter Eight

After quitting work, I spent a long time hanging around the house, a ghost of who I used to be. Mum and Dad were worried about me, but I kept them at arm's length as best I could, avoiding their questions and attempts to make conversation. I didn't want to talk about what was going on; I didn't know where to start.

I was low on money during this time, but I was still managing to drink heavily. Alcohol was the only thing getting me up and out of bed in the mornings, and I spent most of my time either sleeping off a hangover or drinking; either down the local pub, or downing cheap cider in someone's living room. Occasionally I would get lucky and get a day's work with a tradesperson from the pub, or I'd manage to save a tiny amount. When I had a bit of cash I'd get cocaine, but mainly I just got drunk, boozing myself into a mind-numbing sleep as quickly as I could.

One day, I came back from the pub to find Trevor's sister, Doreen, sitting at the table with my mum. I hadn't spent much time with Trevor in the past few years, but he had still been fond of me and my brother, and had kept us both in his thoughts. He'd also been suffering from poor physical health, as well as his ongoing battles with his mental health, and had passed away quietly a few weeks earlier.

This had been a huge deal for me, not because I was particularly sad (or, in fact, sad at all), but because there were rumours that David and I were written into the will. If this sounds cold-hearted and materialistic, it's because it was. I was deep in my own mess, and heavily in debt. I'd run out of avenues to get cash, and I'd bled my mum dry, and, of course, I still needed to buy alcohol to keep me going. Trevor's death had come at the perfect time for me to buy myself out of the mess I'd made.

'Any news?' I'd ask Mum every day. I was a desperate addict, my mind focused on my next source of income, and my next hit.

'We have to wait for his house to be sold, Matt,' Mum told me, and I would groan in frustration.

'Can't they just lower the price?' I would ask, 'Honestly, I'm happy to lose a few thousand, that doesn't matter to me, I just need that money!'

It's embarrassing looking back, how callous I was around the time of Trevor's death. I didn't care that my parents had lost a friend, and I didn't care about how Doreen was holding up after the death of her brother. The only focus of my attention was myself, and I didn't care who knew it.

And then the day arrived. I looked at Doreen sitting at my parent's table, and knew what she'd come to tell me. My heart leapt. I couldn't wait to see how much I was getting.

'Matt,' she said, 'you're one lucky man!'

She slid a cheque across the table. I looked at the number £79,000. My heart skipped a beat.

'Oh my God,' I said.

'That's a third of the house,' said Doreen, 'and you're getting a third of his savings as well. In total it all comes to just over £100,000. The rest will hit your bank account in a few weeks' time.'

I stared at her, unable to believe it. Even in my wildest imaginings I hadn't dared to dream that it would be this much money. I looked up into the air in gratitude, a surge of warmth for Trevor washing over me.

'Thank you, Uncle Trev,' I said quietly. And in that moment I meant it.

'Be careful with that money, won't you?' said Doreen, and I nodded fervently.

'I will,' I said, 'I promise.'

And I did genuinely mean to keep my word, but life kept getting in the way, and there were things I needed to do before I could be sensible. I was ecstatic. I paid off all my debts and loans, including everything I'd borrowed from my mum. I was in the black for the first time in years, and I had tens of thousands left to spare. I felt a sense of freedom that was indescribable; nothing in the world seemed off-limits anymore. I decided that I'd spend a bit, and then I'd save later on. *Tomorrow*, I kept telling myself, *tomorrow I'll be sensible.* Except tomorrow never arrived.

'Why don't you give a bit of it to us, Matt?' said my mum warily, seeing the dollar signs in my eyes, and looking nervously at the shopping bags that were multiplying all over my room. 'We can pop it in a savings account for you, and then you won't just spend it all.'

I said no of course. Why would I save when I could spend? And, anyway, I was sure I had it under control. If I'd been sensible, as Doreen had requested, I could have done so much with the money. I could have got myself on the property ladder. I could have put some in savings accounts as Mum suggested, or bought some shares. If nothing else, I could have gone travelling, or at least taken my mum on a nice holiday. I did none of this.

Instead, I launched out on a ridiculous and frivolous spending spree. I bought every material thing that I could get my hands on, and of course, as much alcohol and cocaine as I needed. I flung cash around left, right and centre, purchasing things I didn't particularly want, and definitely didn't need. I loved the power that the money gave me; I loved the thrill of being able to afford anything I could dream of.

This behaviour went on for months. There was a shop in Cheltenham called Trapeze, famed for its branded clothes and general reputation as a cool place, frequented only by people with money and style. I'd wander in and buy things straight off the racks without even trying them on. If they didn't fit, or I didn't like them, I'd discard them. My bedroom at my parents' house slowly turned into a storage room, with piles of brand new clothes lying in every corner.

It was a similar story with jewellery. I went into every jeweller's within walking distance, and bought handfuls of rings, as well as a chain, a bracelet, a watch, and a St. Christopher pendant. Later on I saw another St. Christopher that was bigger and flashier than the one I had, so I bought that as well.

I would spend my days wandering in and out of shops with my arms full of bags. I bought flashy trainers and high-end gadgets, showing off as much as I could. When I was done shopping for the day, I'd meander from pub to pub with my branded bags on show, keen for people to see that I was richer than I'd ever been before. When I couldn't be bothered to walk, I took taxis, tipping generously, even for a five-minute ride.

'You alright, Matt?' asked one of the drivers once. All the taxi drivers had got to know me, and we regularly chatted on my short trips around Cheltenham.

'Never better, mate,' I said cheerfully. The driver looked at me in the mirror, concerned.

'Be careful with that money,' he said. I just rolled my eyes. I was fine.

Except I wasn't fine. I was drinking more than ever, and using cocaine all day every day. I was also rattling through my money at an impressive speed. As well as my shopping sprees, I was constantly buying people pints and handing out bags of cocaine, determined to be the life and soul of the party. I'd managed to convince myself that I was happy and doing well, but inside, I was still that little boy who craved attention. My mental health was on thin ice, exacerbated by heavy drug use, and I was deeply lonely. Paying for everyone's drinks and drugs in exchange for unlimited company seemed like a fair exchange, and I did it happily.

Perhaps the one sensible decision I made during my period of wild spending was to buy a car. Even so, I bought the flashiest car I could (to impress), for the least amount of money I could (so I could still buy drugs). My BMW cost me £15,000, and I still love it to this day. Nevertheless, I bought the first one I saw with very little research, more worried about the image it gave off than anything else. My decision-making was horrendous, and my carefree attitude towards money was slowly getting me into hot water.

***

I had, until now, managed to stay off the crack, even with all the money rolling round in my bank account. I knew that it had been a lucky escape last time, and that I couldn't go down that road again. I was determined to stick to my word. And then I began hanging around with Taz.

I'd actually met Taz about six months earlier. I'd been invited round to a flat by a complete stranger, just someone I'd met on a night out. I can't remember quite how I ended up there, but I assume I had offered them drugs in order to keep the night going. I sat at this stranger's kitchen table sniffing fat lines of coke that Taz had racked up, and working my way through the stash of booze in the flat. After a while, I sensed Taz's eyes burning into me across the room, and I saw him lean over and speak to his mate, glancing at me as he did so. It wasn't Taz's flat, but it was clear he was at the top of the social hierarchy. It wasn't long before I was ushered out, my presence clearly unwelcome. I figured that we were too similar; we were both loud and boisterous. We also both had a tendency to show off and demand attention, especially when we had substances inside us. I left the house that night not particularly bothered; I hadn't liked him very much either.

Now, six months later, I ran into him in town. I was head to toe in Stone Island, dripping with flashy gold jewellery, and laden down with shopping bags from expensive shops. I was also rake thin and wild-eyed, clearly heavily into drugs for anyone who knew what to look for.

'Matt!' Taz exclaimed, looking me up and down in admiration, 'bloody hell mate, how's it going?'

I looked at him suspiciously. Just a few months ago he'd been unceremoniously booting me out of his mates flat, and now he was treating me like a close friend.

'I thought you hated me...?' I said cautiously.

'Nah, not at all,' he said, 'how's it going? Fancy a pint?'

We went for a drink together, bobbing into the nearest Wetherspoons, and ordering a couple of beers. I paid. Taz didn't offer, and I didn't ask; as per usual, I was just pleased to have someone to drink with. We hit it off completely that day, drinking and sniffing until the evening, chatting the day away.

'Shall we take this back to mine?' Taz asked as the light dimmed, and evening turned into night. I had mountains of cocaine on me, and I was pleasantly full of drink. I felt good about myself, and I was keen to carry the party on.

'Yep,' I said, 'fuck it. Why not?'

Other people joined us in Taz's flat, and the night rapidly turned into a full-on party, with music pumping and the lights turned down low. It was very much like the night when I'd met him six months ago, except this time I was the centre of the party, my presence very much wanted. Suddenly, someone pulled out a crack pipe. I balked.

'Whoa,' I said, 'no, no, no, I can't do that, I used to have a bit of a problem with that stuff.' I shook my head at Taz, remembering how miserable I had been the last time I'd been heavily into crack.

'Nah, come on Matt,' said Taz, laughing at my face, 'we'll be quick. It's nothing serious.' I shook my head again, and, managing to stay strong, headed home.

The next day I was bombarded with text messages from Taz.

You're my brother, he said, *we have a connection.* I felt my resolve weaken, and we arranged to meet up again that day. Deep down I was aware that Taz was just using me for my money. It was pretty clear that his attitude had changed because I could supply him with unlimited drink and drugs. Still, I quashed this thought, unwilling to address it. We had got on well after all, and a friend was a friend.

That day was the same as the one before. We pub-hopped until the evening, flat out on alcohol and cocaine, with me paying for everything. Just like before, as night fell, we ended up back at his flat. This time it was just me and him, and when he asked whether I wanted to smoke crack, I broke. Since the party the night before I'd been unable to think about anything except the high. I was obsessed, delirious at the thought of the pipe, and powerless over the pull.

'Yeah, I'll have a bit,' I said.

'Do you have any coke going spare then, mate?' said Taz, 'I'm going to wash it up.'

'Washing up' is the process of turning cocaine into crack, using bicarbonate of soda, a metal spoon, and a lighter or a tea light. Mixed together and heated, the bicarb and the coke react with each other, and an oily mixture separates from the rest. This is the crack. You scrape it off, cool it, and then smoke the crystals that form. I'd never seen it done before, and I watched, mesmerised.

As Taz scraped off the globules of crack that formed, my brain ticked over. I realised that if I just washed-up cocaine, then no-one would ever have to know that I was back on the crack. Because I was. My mind was made up. I was going to do it.

Washed up crack is much purer than the stuff you buy pre-made from the street. You never really know what's in pre-made crack; it's often been cut with other things to make up the volume. You can often find substances such as aspirin, benzocaine, or even laundry detergent or laxatives in street crack. Washed up crack contains none of this. As a result, it's the purest you can get, and I'd never had a high like it.

We smoked it that night through makeshift crack pipes made from mini vodka bottles, inhaling deeply. I felt like I was being given a warm hug, like someone's arms were wrapped around me and holding me safe, and I floated on a warm cloud of bliss. We smoked all night, interspersing huffs on the crack pipe with packets of cigarettes. We chatted about nothing, watched crappy TV, and laughed until our sides hurt. It was euphoric; I felt like I was walking on air.

I came down to Earth the next day, when I finally began to sober up sometime in the afternoon. I felt sick and miserable, and my lungs were sore from all the smoke.

Never again, Matt, I told myself, *seriously, never again. This has to stop now.*

Of course, by the end of that night I was back at Taz's, my lungs full of crack smoke, riding the high until the morning.

I spiralled again. Each morning I'd wake up and promise myself never again. Then I'd get a bombardment of texts from Taz: *you're like a brother to me*; *you're my best mate.* The attention was irresistible, and I'd crumble.

I slowly slid into an inescapable routine of booze and coke by day and crack by night. Locked up together in his flat, Taz and I would watch mindless TV, giggling uncontrollably. We'd talk in funny accents and shout in each other's faces, every tiny thing suddenly hilarious. The curtains were always shut; we were terrified of the light. Like vampires, we hid in the darkness, staying awake all night, wired and unable to sleep.

Slowly, pounding sunlight would creep through the cracks in the curtains, and we'd sober up, our heads and lungs churning. Without even discussing it, Taz would run to the shop to get us some booze, and then the whole cycle would begin again. I don't know exactly how long I spent in this depressing circular haze of alcohol and narcotics, but it must have been weeks, if not months.

Money was no longer an object, and I didn't work. As a result, there was absolutely nothing to slow me down, or make me consider what I was doing with my life. I ricocheted between pure joy and true misery; from soaring highs straight back down to unbearable lows. All addicts know this feeling well; the drug induced place where there is only good and bad, with nothing in between. I was lost. I felt underwater, and like I was unable to touch the bottom. The only thing I could do to fix it was to take more drugs.

***

People were constantly warning me about Taz. He had a reputation in the local area, and friends I hung around with would pull me to one side at parties and ask what I was doing.

'You know he's using you, right Matty?' they'd say. I blew them all off. I knew they were right, but I actually enjoyed hanging around with Taz. We genuinely got on well, and I wasn't willing to give up on something that felt like true friendship to me.

My parents were still concerned, and I was still avoiding them, spending as much time away from the house as I could. I sofa surfed a lot, crashing with friends whenever I could, and spending my money on hotels when I couldn't, staying up all night and smoking crack in the rooms.

Every time it got too bad mentally, I would come crawling back home, usually looking worse for wear and clutching several expensive shopping bags full of unnecessary goods. It was evident that I was blowing through my money at an increasingly rapid speed, and Mum and Dad were at a complete loss; they truly didn't know what to do.

'You need psychiatric help, Matt, this isn't normal,' my mum screamed at me once, near tears. She wanted to help me but didn't know what to do.

'I'm fine,' I insisted, 'I've still got loads of my money left. Stop overreacting!'

Every time things got too emotional at home, I'd storm out again, staying away and binging for another few nights.

Then things began to turn with Taz. No matter how hard I tried to ignore the fact that he was using me, it was becoming impossible to avoid. He'd become increasingly confident in his power over me, and was using me in more obvious ways.

He'd talk to girls and get them to pretend they fancied me so I'd supply them with drinks all night. He also began to change his tactics in order to get money out of me.

One time I was round his. There were five of us; three lads and two girls. Taz took me to one side and spoke to me in a low voice.

'Mate, the girls were robbed earlier today. They haven't got any money for a taxi. Someone took £50 off them!'

'Mate, that's so shit,' I said, 'who took it?

'I dunno, one of their friends I think?'

'Let me know who did it, and I'll sort it out.' I'd meant that I'd get involved, and that I'd talk to whoever had taken it. Instead, I received a text message with a set of bank details and a cheerful thank you. I didn't send any cash. It was clear I was just being used for my money.

What I didn't realise at first is that Taz had orchestrated the entire plan.

'I hate those two for what they did to you,' he said to me afterwards, shaking his head. It never even occurred to me that he'd been the brains behind the whole thing. Still, I could feel that our relationship was shifting, that there was a change in the power dynamics. I was headed for serious trouble, and I could feel it in my gut.

Chapter Nine

I was descending deeper and deeper into my crack habit; my world was a messy tangle of terrible decisions and expensive clothes. By the winter of 2018, barely a couple of months after I'd received the money, I'd spent nearly half of it. I knew I needed to break free of Taz somehow. I was self-aware enough to realise that he was a corrupting influence on me, and that things were only going to get worse while he was living in my pocket. I just didn't know how to pull away from him.

One November morning we peered round the curtains to bright, sparkling winter sunshine. We'd been on a two- or three-day crack binge, and we were wired, gunning for some excitement.

'Spoons?' suggested Taz, and I started putting my shoes on. I needed something else in my bloodstream me to bring me down, and I knew alcohol would do the job. We were also out of drugs by that point, and booze was the only substance available easily at 8am.

We wandered down Cheltenham high street in the frosty morning light, talking loudly. Taz stole a pasty from Greggs, and then we went to the pub, knocking back a few pints. We chatted about nothing, the conversation drifting, and we eventually found our way back to drug talk, as we always did.

'Shall we get some coke?' said Taz, 'we can wash it up tonight.'

'Always mate,' I replied. I knocked back the remainder of my pint and stood up, pulling out my phone to text my regular dealer.

As we headed home, Taz darted into a toy shop, and came out minutes later wielding a plastic rifle. It's worth mentioning that Taz was always keen to shoplift, even when he was at his most sober. When he was high or pissed (and therefore full of confidence) there was virtually nothing he wouldn't take. His self-assurance and lack of nerves actually made him quite an effective thief, and no-one questioned him as he darted out of the toy shop on that morning, ripping the tags off his stolen toy gun.

It was about 11am by now, and the high street was rammed with people Christmas shopping. The Cheltenham Races were on as well, and it had turned into a beautiful day; the whole town was bustling, and we were brimming with excitement. We began to play with the gun, running up and down and pretending to shoot each other.

Our game was a bit of fun, it's important to note. We never had any real desire to scare anyone. Nevertheless, we began aiming the gun at passers-by, laughing, hiding, and rolling around, pretending we were in combat.

As we ran past John Lewis, a security guard caught sight of us, and, unbeknown to us, called the police. CCTV then followed us through town, where they caught me banging on the window of a Starbucks, laughing like a madman. I pointed the rifle through the glass at a couple drinking coffee and shouted 'PEW PEW', giggling manically.

The game lost its appeal quickly, and we headed to the bus station to go and meet the dealer, unaware that we were being watched, and completely oblivious to the chaos we'd set in motion.

'Here, hold this,' said Taz, chucking the gun to me. He fished a packet of cigarettes out of his pocket, and went to light one. Suddenly, there was movement behind us, a swift flash of someone moving at high speed. I heard a shout.

'Armed police, stay where you are, turn around slowly!'

I swivelled as instructed, and came face to face with a policeman brandishing a Taser.

'What the fuck are you on about?' I said, just as three police cars screeched up, surrounding us. I gawped at the policeman, unable to believe what was happening.

'Get on the ground now! On your knees!' shouted the policeman.

I went down as instructed, suddenly terrified, still clutching the plastic gun in one hand.

'SLIDE THE GUN ACROSS THE FLOOR TO ME SLOWLY,' yelled the policeman.

'How am I supposed to do that slowly?' I shrieked back. For once, I wasn't trying to be funny, I just genuinely didn't want to get into any more trouble.

'JUST DO IT!' was the response. I slid the gun as best as I could, the plastic skittering across the concrete slabs. There was quite a crowd gathering by now; people emerging from the pubs to see what was going on. A few taxi drivers had climbed out of their cabs, and I saw a few of them filming us on their phones, laughing as the police cuffed me and Taz.

'I could have shot you dead then,' the policeman said to me as he escorted me to the pavement to wait for the police van. I was still tipsy, and I felt cocky and sure of myself as a result.

'Bet you wish you did!' I replied. I was enjoying myself now; I felt like the star of a gritty police drama, and I was loving the attention. And then I remembered something. My heart plummeted. I had coke in my pocket – barely hidden – and I was just about to be taken into a police station, where I'd almost certainly be searched. *Fuck*, I thought, *THINK, Matt.*

''Scuse me mate?' I asked the policeman, 'can you just uncuff me so I can grab a fag? I'll be a nightmare in the cells otherwise.'

'I'll get you one,' said the policeman, to my horror, 'where are they? In your pocket?'

I had no choice but to nod and allow him to reach into my pocket. Incredibly, he managed to find my cigarettes and lighter, pull them both out, and then put them back in without discovering the coke. I sat, cuffed, waiting for the police van, with a cigarette in my mouth, feeling both relieved that I'd not been caught yet, and terrified by what was to come.

By the time we got to Gloucester police station the seriousness of what I'd done had hit me. I could feel my heart beating, and the blood pumping round my veins as they searched me, every inch of me silently begging them not to find the coke. It worked. They didn't. But I had sobered up enough by now to realise that I had made a real mess for myself. I remember standing at the custody desk, and pulling off every single one of my flashy gold rings, dropping them quietly into the tray, while watching Taz being processed over the other side of the desk. We were in serious trouble, and I knew it.

We'd travelled to the police station separately, and we were interviewed separately, so we didn't have time to come up with a story together. The officer slid a piece of paper across the desk to me. It was a photo of Taz's rifle.

'Can you tell me what this is, Matthew?' he asked.

'It's a plastic gun,' I said quietly.

'Can you tell me where you got this?'

'My friend bought it,' I said, still staying loyal to Taz. I didn't want to tell the police that he'd stolen the toy.

'What were you doing with it?'

'I was just being an idiot,' I said, with real shame in my voice. The officer looked at me carefully.

'Off the record, you've been a bit of a twat, haven't you?' he said sternly.

For the millionth time in my life, my charm worked, and I was released without charge later that day. Taz got a bit more of a serious telling off, but was also released with no further action.

We met up outside, utterly elated, both of us carrying plastic bags with our belongings in. We couldn't believe our luck.

'Pub?' suggested Taz.

'Pub!' I agreed. It was time to celebrate.

It was late evening by now, so we got a taxi to a local pub and began drinking again, telling our story to anyone who would listen. I was buying drinks for everyone in sight, celebrating my lucky escape.

People at home had heard what had happened as well; I got a message from my cousin later that night.

What have you been up to? he said.

Not much I typed back.

You liar.

My phone pinged again, and suddenly I was watching a video of myself that someone had filmed from the Municipal Offices in town. It was clear that everyone knew, and I felt strangely proud of myself.

We headed home on the bus later that night, and Taz tried to persuade me to carry on the party. He was riding the high of the day, and yet I suddenly felt overwhelmed and drained.

'I can't mate,' I said, 'I'm so exhausted.'

'Aw come on mate,' he said, 'laundry?' Laundry was our code word for washing up crack, used when other people were in earshot.

'I just need to go home, Taz,' I said, and for once I put my foot down. He looked visibly pissed off, but there was nothing he could do.

Dad picked me up from the bus station, none the wiser to what had gone on. I knew it was only a matter of time before he found out, so I turned to him in the car.

'Dad, I've got something really stupid to tell you.' I didn't mention the crack, but I told him everything else, making it out to be a humorous misunderstanding. With no charge or consequences, he didn't seem concerned, and the whole thing was rapidly forgotten. Once again, I'd avoided serious trouble by the skin of my teeth.

***

The more time I spent hanging around with Taz, the less I was washing up, and the more I was buying street crack.

I realised that I was beginning to develop a really problematic habit, and I needed to get away from Taz – not necessarily to get off the drugs, but to stop paying for his habit as well.

One of the final straws in the breaking of our relationship was the suit incident. For some reason I had always had my heart set on a carefully fitted suit that had been measured to me perfectly. One day, Taz and I struck a deal. I was going to go to a fancy suit shop and choose a suit that I loved, and then Taz was going to shoplift it for me, and then sell it back to me at half the rack price. This was his idea of doing me a favour, and the closest he ever got to lending me money, or paying for anything for me.

On the day we were due to pull off our scheme, I didn't feel right about it. Something in my gut told me it was the wrong thing to do, and I felt very uncomfortable going through with our plan. The man in the shop was so nice; he measured me up carefully, and together we picked out a suit I loved. He took it up to the till for me, and I headed up with Taz, pulling out my wallet.

'What are you doing, mate?' he hissed at me. I shook my head at him.

'I can't, Taz, he's a sound bloke. He probably gets commission on this sort of stuff as well!'

'Nah, mate, don't buy it. I'll rob it. I need the money anyway!'

Something in me stopped me letting Taz steal the suit for me, and I paid for it, feeling the heat of Taz's glare on me the entire time.

When we got outside, I could tell that Taz was furious. I could also tell that he was in two minds about what to do. If he beat me up then our friendship would be over forever – but then so would his supply of drugs.

I made a decision after that. It was time to cut Taz out of my life, and rapidly. I'd told him over and over again that I couldn't smoke crack anymore, and that life was getting too chaotic and scary for me. He always laughed it off, and I struggled to ever say no to him.

Of course, I was far too cowardly to break up our friendship in person, so I effectively ghosted him; I began to reply to his messages in single words, slowly cutting out the replies altogether. In a strike of good timing, he went to prison shortly afterwards. He'd knocked someone out in a fight, and then robbed them while they lay in the street. I was very aware it could easily have been me, had I got on the wrong side of him. I felt lucky to be free.

Somehow, without Taz egging me on, I managed to stop smoking crack again briefly. It was Christmastime, and although I was still using coke and drinking heavily, I recognized that I was on the edge, and my mind and body needed a break from the crack.

My quitting didn't stop any tension at home. Mum and Dad could see that I was falling, and their questioning and worrying increased.

'What's going on Matt? Are you on drugs?' Mum asked me once, 'I think you need to talk to someone urgently. A psychiatrist or a doctor or someone. Please will you get some help?'

This would have been the perfect time to open up and to get some real support, but I wasn't able to. I didn't feel ready, and, once again, I didn't know where to begin. Instead, I blew her off.

'Of course I'm not on drugs, Mum!' I snapped, running away from the conversation once again.

***

I moved out of the family home. I could see that I was breaking my mum and dad's hearts, and I wanted to get away. Looking back now, this was just me taking storming out to the next level. I was just keen to get away from the questions, and the concern that followed me from room to room at my parents'.

I went flat hunting, and rented the first one I saw, paying a year's rent up front to get round my terrible credit rating and the fact I didn't have a job. The flat was in a beautiful building in a really smart area of town. I loved the way my shiny car looked parked outside it. That was where the beauty ended; inside it was horrible.

In my defence, I did try at first. *This is a fresh start*, I told myself once again as I got the keys. I bought a whole load of second-hand furniture and made the inside as cosy as I could for as cheap as I could. I even had one of those *you've made it Matt* moments again on my first night, eating a sandwich in front of my TV.

Unfortunately, this feeling didn't last long. I was delusional about my ability to cope, still drinking heavily, and things fell apart very quickly. Being at home with my parents had been my last real thread keeping me held down to Earth, and without it I was completely lost, floating free in a haze. I'd been in the flat for about a week when I washed some coke up into crack, just because there was nothing stopping me.

That was the beginning of the end. I totally lost control, and for the first time, things inside my head became incredibly scary. I began to see things, my eyes chasing shadows that weren't there, convinced that people were inside my flat with me. I was incredibly paranoid, and began keeping a knife with me at all times, running to the door and brandishing it when I thought I heard people outside.

I became convinced that I was being watched, and I'd army crawl under the windows to avoid being seen by the prying eyes that I was sure were out there. Even when I was lying alone in the dark, I didn't feel safe. I was convinced that drones were coming in through the windows, and I would constantly check, twitching the curtains and gazing out into the night.

Even when I wasn't paranoid, my behaviour was weird. I'd listen to the same songs on repeat, over and over and over until they were burned into my brain. Sometimes I'd bark like a dog, and laugh about it, sniggering alone in my dark living room. I didn't eat, and I barely slept, passing out at any hour of the day or night, when I became too exhausted to stay awake a moment longer.

I became somewhat withdrawn from society, apart from regular trips to the pub. When I met with dealers, I always got them to bring the drugs straight to my door. I was terrified of the normal world, pushing away all my good friends who wouldn't get high or drunk with me. I'd cut them out as soon as they showed any signs of disapproval, or even mentioned that I might need some help. I just didn't want to hear it.

One of the good friends I pushed away was Deb. Our friendship never reached the level it had been in the earlier years, but we were once again on speaking terms. Nevertheless, I kept her at arm's length. As she'd never been keen on drugs, I didn't want her to find out how bad things had become for me. I stopped the friendship blossoming into what it had been; I just didn't want someone else to try and intervene.

Despite shoving all my true friends away, I still craved company. Unsure of how else to get people to hang out with me, I began to tempt people over to my flat. I would offer them drugs and money just so I wasn't alone.

Lucy's little brother, Harrison, came back into my life, and initially latched on to me like Taz did. He would bombard me with texts like Taz had, claiming we had a connection, and saying that we were best friends, and we needed to stick together. I was flattered, and I welcomed the attention. I'd buy him cigarettes whenever he needed them, and provided him with drugs on tap, enjoying his company and the break from my own thoughts.

111

When the money began to run out, things began to change. He'd refuse to come over if I had nothing left to give him.

'I've bought you loads, Harri,' I'd say, pleading with him, 'you owe me money if anything!'

'That's your own fault,' he laughed, 'shouldn't have blown through that £100k so quickly, should you?'

One night, desperate for company, I paid for his taxi to come over. I was a complete mess at this point, barely able to move from the sofa. Harrison saw that I was in a state, and quickly made his excuses to leave, saying goodbye to me with a huge grin on his face. It was only later that I found out he'd robbed me, taking all my remaining drugs, and any cash he could get his hands on. I didn't even really care. I carried on paying for people to come and see me, determined to never be alone, and to never stop using.

This slow and self-destructive meltdown went on for a long time. My behaviour was at best reckless, and at worst downright dangerous. I nearly set the flat on fire several times, burning the carpet while smoking, or falling asleep with a cigarette in my hand. I'd jacked up all my lighters for the crack spoon and once I set my trousers on fire when I misjudged the height of the flame. I was half passed out, and barely able to move. I sleepily put the fire out with my sock, dabbing at it until it was extinguished. Then I fell asleep, luckily completely unhurt.

The flat was slowly becoming a disgusting hovel. I never tidied or even washed up; I could often be found drinking whiskey out of cereal bowls because I couldn't be bothered to clean a cup. I was a mess as well; I'd have to hold the bowls with two hands while I drank because I was shaking so violently.

My inheritance money was almost completely gone by this time. I began gambling again, hoping madly that I'd manage to win some back. I was telling my mum that I still had loads left, unable to admit to her how stupid I was, and how insane I'd been.

Unbelievably, I managed to get a job towards the end of this period. A friend from the pub was looking for a warehouse assistant and I applied, telling myself once again that this was a fresh start and a chance to sort myself out.

I didn't even try. I was using drugs at work from the very beginning, including crack. I was there for two months, and I cannot remember a single full day. I was permanently out of it, floating on a sick cloud of narcotics. I was also physically weak, and running on absolute fumes. It was a tough manual job, and in the hot sun with an empty stomach I often felt unbearably unwell. I was regularly sent home, or called in sick, and on the days I did work, I was barely useful.

***

I spent the last £1000 of my inheritance money in a roulette machine, just six months after I had got it. I fed that £1000 in £10 notes into the machine, over and over until it was completely gone. And that was it. Not a single penny was left, and I couldn't tell a soul. I felt completely sick, and utterly hopeless. I had no idea what to do.

I still had a good stash of drugs that I carted round in a Kinder egg. At a loss as to what else to do, I went into the toilets at Ladbrokes and smoked a pipe, nauseous with fear. I then bought a bottle of whiskey, went home, got out a payday loan, and carried on spending.

I felt on the edge of sheer panic, like I couldn't breathe properly anymore. At the same time, I was still stuck in a horrible cycle of booze, drugs and spending, and I didn't know how to break out of it. I shook down all my furniture, desperately searching for small change, coming up with a handful of silver that would just about buy me a pint.

I walked to the pub, shaking and sweating, withdrawing horribly from the alcohol, and needing something to take the anxiety away. They refused me service. It was clear that I was broken. I bought a bottle and went home instead.

Later on, I got in my car and drove down to the pub. It was a two-minute walk, but I was too exhausted to face it. I had a pipe in the toilets and then drank two whiskey and cokes in swift succession, needing an anaesthetic for the pain in my head.

I was driving back home that night when I saw the familiar blue lights flashing in my rear view mirror. *Fuck it*, I thought, *I can make it home*. I pulled into my driveway with the police following me, knowing I was about to be breathalysed, and knowing that it was likely that I'd be over the limit. I couldn't bring myself to care. I had reached a level of panic and hopelessness so huge that I felt completely numb.

I was over the limit, but only slightly. Still, I was taken down to the station, and spent the rest of the night in the cells. I didn't care. They hadn't found the crack pipe in my car, and I just about had enough energy left in me to be relieved about that. The rest of my emotions had gone.

I was let out of the cells later that morning, and I managed to stagger into work, blurry from lack of sleep. I was constantly caught between being too wiped-out to care about the mess I was in, and caring so much that I was sick with anxiety. My solution to save face in my miserable state was to pretend with all my might that nothing in the world worried me. It was exhausting.

'Yeah, got caught drink driving last night, didn't I?' I told everyone in a desperate bid for admiration. My boss was less than impressed.

'You're an idiot,' he said, 'you're going to get banned, you know?'

I didn't know. My heart sank, but, as ever, I pretended not to care.

He was right of course. I was banned from driving for a year, and given a drink driving course to go on. It was a real shock to me, another huge crack in the crumbling mess of my life. Once again, of course, I played the cocky fool, turning up at court half-drunk, with an entourage of mates to chivvy me along. I was sniggering as the judge sentenced me, my laughter barely masking the pain I was in inside.

Chapter Ten

In July 2019 I finally reached the end. The end of the line. The end of my tether. The end of my willingness to live like I was anymore. I gave in. I suddenly realised that what was going on in my head was bigger than I was able to cope with, and that it was growing at a terrifying pace. I finally grasped, with absolute clarity that I needed serious help, and I needed it quickly. All I had to do was ask for it.

I took my phone out of my pocket and brought up my mum's number, staring at it on the screen. It was such a small act, but it seemed huge. I could barely even make sense of my problems in my own head, let alone explain it to someone else. But there was nothing else left that I could do. Summoning all the strength I had, I took a deep breath and hit call.

'Matt,' she said, her voice full of fear, 'are you okay?'

'No, Mum,' I said, 'I really need to talk to you. Can I come home for a bit?'

'Of course,' Mum said, 'whenever you want.'

That was mid-afternoon, and I finally headed home at about 11pm. I'd spent the afternoon holed up in my flat with a bottle of whisky, downing it for Dutch courage. I'd also sniffed a lot of coke and smoked a lot of crack so I didn't appear too drunk. I knew I needed to explain what was going on, but I couldn't bring myself to do it.

Mum was in bed when I finally stumbled in through the door, and I headed up the stairs to see her. She sat up in bed when she heard me come in, and I sat down on the stool she uses to put her make up on. For a while we just looked at each other through the dark. And then I began to tell the truth.

'I'm addicted to crack cocaine, Mum,' I said, 'I need help.'

I told her how long it had been going on, and how much I was doing. I told her about the money, and the fact that I was in debt again. I told her about the cocaine and the drinking. I told her about the mess my flat was in, and how scared I was. Throughout it all she sat and listened, tears pouring silently down her face. I began to choke up towards the end, but mainly I felt emotionless. I was completely numbed by all the substances, unable to feel anything at all.

'What do you need, Matt?' asked Mum when I'd finally finished talking.

'I need to go to rehab,' I said.

'Are you really that bad?' she said. I looked at her, amazed. I couldn't believe how well I'd managed to keep everything hidden.

'Yes,' I said, my voice thick with tears, 'I am that bad. I really am, and I don't know what to do. Could you research some places for me? Rehabs I mean?'

'Yes,' she said, 'of course. Will you stay here tonight?' The pain in her eyes was evident, but I couldn't spend another minute there.

'No,' I said, 'I've got a friend at mine, and I can't leave him there. I may as well stay at mine.' Mum looked at me carefully.

'Are you going to take drugs, Matt?' she asked. I didn't know what to say, but I didn't want to lie anymore. I shrugged.

'What do you want me to say, Mum?' I asked, getting up to leave. On some level, I think Mum appreciated the honesty. I headed home that night utterly broken, but relieved on some level. There seemed a little glimmer of hope, even though I was in no way out of the woods.

The few days after that conversation are a blur. I know that at some point, Mum chose a rehab in Runcorn called Oasis, and arranged for me to have an assessment phone call.

'A man called Anthony is going to call you,' she told me, 'and you have to be sober. You can't miss this conversation.'

I did manage to answer the phone when Anthony rang, and I answered all his questions while he assessed me for a place. I also managed to stay sober, but the whole time I was on the phone I was dreaming about using.

'Okay Matt,' said Anthony, 'we'll see you soon. Stay safe.'

And with that, my place at rehab was booked. I felt a sick combination of relief and nervousness. It was unbearable, so I drowned it in more drugs and booze.

I went to work the next day to give my one week's notice. I was rake thin, my complexion pasty, and stinking of alcohol, shaking like a leaf as I stood there. My boss took me into a private room when I gave my notice, and asked how I was doing. He knew that I drank too much, and that I took a lot of coke, but when I mentioned the fact that I'd been on crack, his face fell.

'Crack!? Bloody hell, Matt. Yeah, go home right now' he said, 'I accept your resignation with immediate effect. You need help, mate, and I'm glad you're getting it.'

I had just been banned from driving, of course, so I walked home, feeling like another weight had been lifted.

I don't want to make it seem like the lead up to rehab was all ease and sunshine. Although the weight of the secrecy was lifted from my shoulders, I was still in a dark place, and in some ways, things got much worse. I had stopped trying to battle my demons now that professional help was in sight. As a result, my drug use ramped up significantly. The week before rehab I sold all my furniture, scrabbling together every penny I could, and buying as much drink and as many drugs as I could possibly afford. My mum knew the extent of my habit by now, and she was terrified for me.

'Please be careful, love,' she would beg me on the phone. Selfishly, I waved her concerns away. I just wanted to be alone.

I spent that week sat in my empty flat, smoking crack and drinking, while sat on the dirty carpet, surrounded by nothing but empty bottles. I went deep into my own head, wallowing in a mess of self-pity and darkness. I felt completely and utterly alone. In that moment, though, that was exactly how I wanted to feel. I wanted one last blowout; one last descent into the misery of addictive behaviour.

***

On the 18th July 2019 I finally went to rehab. I arrived back at my parents' house at about 2am on the morning I was due to go. I hadn't planned, packed, or remotely prepared at all. In fact, I was doing my best not to think about it. I was still wobbly with drink and foggy from crack as I clambered into the car to leave.

Mum and Dad took me together, both in a show of support for me, and to cling to each other. It must have been horrendous for them, but I was too tired to notice. I sat in the back seat of the car, curled into an awkward and uncomfortable sleep, shaking and sick from my comedown.

The journey took just over two hours, and I slept for most of it, drifting in and out. I vaguely remember my dad getting lost at one point; the sat nav took them the wrong way. I have little memory other than that, and before I knew it, we were in Runcorn, parking in front of Oasis.

The building was nothing like I'd expected. In my mind, rehab was like a posh hotel. I'd expected a stately home type building, with extensive grounds, and maybe some running water and a few swans dotted about. Oasis just looked like a house, or a plain commercial building, parked straight in the centre of town. Even in my withered state I had the audacity to feel slightly disappointed.

'Here we go then, Matt,' said Mum, as we got out the car. I bit my lip and nodded. I was so tired I could barely even speak.

Mum pressed the buzzer, and we heard movement from within the building. Suddenly the door opened and a friendly looking man with a lanyard popped his head out. He grinned cheerfully at us.

'Hi there,' he said, 'someone will be with you in about 20 minutes if that's okay?'

'Course,' said Mum, as cheerfully as she could. The door slammed shut again and we were left waiting outside in a painful and silent limbo. None of us knew what to do. In my nervous state, I chain smoked about four cigarettes, sucking the smoke down as quickly as I could. My lungs were painful from all the crack I'd been smoking, but I didn't know what else to do to pass the time. I coughed and gagged and forced the smoke into my lungs anyway.

At 11am, the door swung open again, and a different man came out, also smiling cheerfully.

'Matt?' he said, looking at me, and I nodded, unable to speak. 'I'm Terry,' he continued, sticking his hand out in greeting, 'welcome to Oasis Runcorn.'

Dad got my bags out of the car, and we all shuffled awkwardly inside.

'Right then, I'll give you all a quick tour, shall I?' said Terry.

'Yes,' said Mum, 'please, that would be nice.'

We walked together down a small corridor into a big room full of tables. There were urns at one end, and coffee and tea, and a big whiteboard on the wall at the other end.

'This is the canteen,' said Terry, 'it's empty at the moment because everyone's in group, but soon it'll be full of activity. This is where you eat, and it's the communal space for activities as well.'

He took us out of a different door, and into a sunny courtyard. At one end it was surrounded by residential buildings, and at the other there were two log cabins. In the middle there was a grassy area, and a rock garden. Flowers lined the walls.

'This is lovely,' said Mum encouragingly. I just nodded. I felt dazed; I couldn't appreciate my surroundings at that moment.

'This is where you'll spend most of your time when the weather is nice,' said Terry, 'the cabins are for groups, and behind us is where you all live. Laundry room is just underneath, and the doctor's office is up there, behind the first cabin.'

'Where do we put the bags?' asked Dad.

'Ah, bring them back this way. The office is on the way out, and no offence Mr and Mrs Ingram, but I'm going to have to ask you to leave now.'

We headed back the way we'd come, winding through the canteen and the corridor, and out into the warm July air at the front of the building. Mum looked at me, her eyes filling up with tears. A pang of guilt hit me in the gut.

'Don't cry, Mum,' I said, reaching out to her.

'Yes, I will bloody cry,' she snapped back fiercely.

'No,' I stammered, 'I didn't mean it like that, I just mean that you'll set me off.' She nodded, and swallowed, then hugged me back.

'I love you so much,' she said.

Dad was much more stoic. He squeezed both my arms, and looked at me in the eyes.

'You can do this, son,' he said. And that was that. My parents climbed into their car, and Terry escorted me back inside, his arm flung around my shoulders.

119

'Everything's going to be alright now, Matt,' he said. I couldn't bring myself to look back.

Terry took me to the office, and we went through a rigorous check-in process. There were pages and pages to sign, and rules to follow, and disclaimers to acknowledge, and I felt like I was barely taking it in. I signed it all anyway, scrawling my name over and over. Then Terry pulled out a pair of gloves and began to put them on. I looked at him, horrified.

'Are you going to check me... you know... for smuggling?' I asked nervously. Terry threw his head back and roared with laughter.

'No mate, this is just so I don't get any of your urine on my hands. I'm going to piss test you!' he laughed. I breathed a sigh of relief.

The urine analysis didn't show up anything unexpected; I was positive for cocaine and nothing else. I was also breathalysed and blew zero.

'Right, mate, that's it,' said Terry, 'I'll come and grab you when the doctor arrives.'

We headed back along the corridor and into the canteen, which now, to my horror, was full of people. I felt anxiety wash into me as four men approached me. Summoning the last bit of strength I had in me, I puffed up my chest and gave them a dirty look. I'd been so used to people using me for my money and my drugs that I automatically assumed that people wanted something from me. I saw everyone as an enemy. Luckily, everyone at rehab had my best interests at heart.

'Hi!' said one of them, 'I'm Jason, and this is Paul, Alan and Umar. Welcome! How are you doing?'

I exhaled in relief. That moment was huge for me; it felt like I could finally let my guard down and focus on getting better.

Another moment of relief came when I saw the doctor. I told him everything, not leaving out a single moment of my history. It was the first time I had ever spilled my story like this, and the doctor sat and listened, nodding kindly, as if nothing I said was surprising to him. As a rehab doctor, it probably wasn't! It felt validating, and again I had that moment of feeling like I was at home.

That's not to say that I didn't feel slightly unsettled. That first afternoon at Oasis felt very strange, and I felt constantly on the verge of being overwhelmed. This wasn't helped by the fact I felt so ill. I was still on a comedown, exhausted and barely clinging on to my sanity.

When it came to lunch, I found I had no appetite, despite not having eaten for weeks. I joined the queue in the canteen and stared at the spread of food in front of me. There was pasta, soup, salad, various meats and cheeses, and the thought of eating even a bite of any of it was too much to contend with.

'I'm sorry,' I said to Danny, the chef, when I got to the front of the queue, 'I just can't... I really can't.' Danny looked at me kindly.

'Just try some soup,' he said, 'we'll get your appetite back in no time,'

I took a bowl of soup and sat at a table, forcing it down. It was pea and ham, but I couldn't taste anything. It felt like my tongue had turned into cotton wool, and I felt nauseous. I managed about half the bowl before I pushed it away.

I sat in the smoking area after dinner looking round at everyone, trying to suss everyone out. I wanted to work out where I'd fit in, and how I would make friends. In the end though, I was too tired to think anymore. I stubbed my cigarette out and headed up to bed.

***

I slept a lot for a few days, except for when they woke me to give me my detox medication. The whole experience had been so utterly overwhelming that my body just craved rest. I'd also been depriving myself of sleep for a very long time; a few days of doing utterly nothing was long overdue.

Oasis was divided into 'flats', little blocks of rooms housing four or five people in total, with a shared living room and bathrooms. Most of the bedrooms were shared rooms, and for the first night I had a roommate called Norman. I remember very little about him; I was just so exhausted. I couldn't even be bothered to unpack; I just crawled into bed and slept.

I was due to share that room for a week, before moving into a room of my own. Luckily for me, another client left early, and

I was allowed to move into his room. I loved it instantly. It was small, but it was clean and tidy, and it was my own space. It backed out onto the garden and the smoking area, and for the rest of my time there I'd look out of the window in the early morning and feel grateful to be there.

Our flat had the 'show' living room, the one that was in all the brochures and website pictures, and the one that was shown to all prospective clients if they came for a look around. It was lovely. I'd sometimes hang around in there in the evenings with my flatmates.

After a few days spent sleeping, someone knocked on my bedroom door. It was Paul.

'Are you coming to group, Matt?' he asked.

'Um, yeah? I guess?' I said. It hadn't really occurred to me that I needed to show up for anything in rehab. I'd sort of hoped that I would get better through osmosis and plenty of sleep. Unfortunately, this was not to be.

Oasis offered two pathways towards recovery: the 12 Step programme, or something called Strengths that was essentially a course of tools for normal living in the outside world.

When I'd been checking in, Terry had asked me to choose.

'I don't know,' I'd said, my brain foggy and exhausted, 'which one is better?'

'Well, I work a 12 Step program,' said Terry, 'and it has worked for me. I'd recommend you go with that.' And so, I did, too tired to debate the pros and cons of each with him.

Two days later, someone asked me which group I was in.

'Um, Steps?' I said nervously, unsure of people's opinions on that. It was a mixed reaction. Half the room groaned, muttering 'Bible basher', and rolling their eyes. The other half cheered.

'Come with us!' said one of them, 'it's honestly the best way to get better.'

Steps had fewer people in the group at the time, so we were in the smaller of the two cabins in the garden. It was the height of summer, and the heat was astounding. We'd been provided with one small fan which blew hot air around the room, and I sat in the corner, slightly confused about what I was doing. Eventually, we were joined by a therapist, Louise.

'Morning all,' she said, smiling round the room, 'and welcome, Matt! Today is actually really special, because Derek is going to be reading us his Step One.'

I had no idea what this meant, but I sat down to listen. Derek turned to face the group. He was older than me, white haired and solid-looking.

'Hi everyone,' he said, 'I'm Derek, I'm an alcoholic, and, um, I'm reading out my Step One today...'

'Hi Derek,' the room chorused. I looked around in confusion.

'So, um, Step One is about admitting I'm powerless. I've answered all these questions about how powerless I am, and I've written down some experiences that, I guess, illustrate that? So, um, I'll just read it out?'

Louise nodded encouragingly, and, slightly nervously, Derek began to read. His story was incredible, and I sat, mesmerized, for the half an hour he was talking. He told us about his life in the Army, and all his missions and deployments. He told us about the Falklands War, and how it had felt to fight; the horrors he saw, and the guilt he carried after that. He then talked about the PTSD that he'd dealt with for years afterwards, and how he'd slid into abusing alcohol to cope.

The whole time I was listening, I felt like I identified with him. Although his route to rehab was so different to mine, I could see how our responses to stressful situations had been very similar. I found myself nodding along as he spoke. It truly felt like things were clicking into place.

'That was amazing, Derek,' I said when I got the chance to feed back to him, 'I feel like I understand so much of what you've been through. I feel like I'm in the right place. Like people will understand me here.' I looked around to see everyone nodding at me, and I quickly looked away, suddenly feeling emotional.

At the end of the session Louise stood up, and everyone held hands.

'God,' she said, and the room began speaking together.

'Grant me the serenity to accept the things I cannot change, the courage to change the things I can, and the wisdom to know the difference. Keep coming back. It works if you work it, so work it – you're worth it!'

There were cheers and hugs and applause, and although in some ways I felt lost and confused, I also felt strongly like I belonged. *This is quite nice*, I thought, *even if it is a bit weird.*

The Steps group, over the time I was in Oasis, took me through the first three Steps of the Alcoholics Anonymous program.

The first step is about surrender: We admitted that we were powerless over alcohol, and that our lives had become unmanageable. While I was happy to admit that my life had become unmanageable, I was less willing to admit my powerlessness at first.

'Crack was my issue,' I argued with Louise on one of the first sessions, 'of course I can still drink.' The idea of not having a drink with my friends was very scary to me. I really wanted to retain some sense of normality when I returned home, and I just didn't see how I could do this without drink in my system.

'But Matt,' said Louise, 'drinking always led you to drugs. What makes you think that you can control that side of you now?'

'I just know I can. I want to be able to drink. How can I have a normal life otherwise?'

Eventually, through more conversations along this vein, I gained some acceptance. I eventually left rehab accepting that I would never drink again, and happy in this knowledge.

Group sessions also allowed us to explore our past away from the 12 Steps, in traditional group therapy. One of the first things I did in this session was write my life story. This was supposed to be a therapeutic activity that allowed us to get out all our history on paper with no alterations. I thought no-one would care, so I kept mine short, skipping out all the using days. As my time at rehab went on, however, I found myself opening up more and more in group therapy. Towards the end of my time, I had addressed enough of my issues to feel comfortable taking pen to paper again. This time, however, it was to write to my parents.

Dear Mum and Dad, I wrote,

I would like to start this letter by saying I love you both very much. That will never change.

I am truly sorry for everything I have done in my life and the unnecessary pain I have caused you. I am blessed to have you both as parents. You have shown me unconditional love through the most difficult times - all of which have been down to my stupidity and selfishness.

Please be assured that my criminal activity, drinking and drug-taking is not a reflection on your parenting. In fact, it is the complete opposite. You couldn't have done anything different to prevent that. I suppose it's just me. I can blame my car accident all I want, and yes it may have played a massive part, but I was hardly the perfect son before that. I'm no psychiatrist but I think my head has always been different. My biggest regret has been not showing you the love that you have shown me. I've been horrible. We do have some happy memories but nowhere near enough - again my fault.

Since coming into treatment I've learnt a great deal about myself. Some stuff I discovered on my own and other stuff from people/staff here. The biggest issue is obviously my drug addiction. I have learnt from treatment that addiction is an illness. The "big book" has taught me this. It's an illness that is never going to go away. But it will be manageable if I follow the steps I am learning here. Rehab isn't a magic cure that will make my illness disappear. Although it would be nice, it just doesn't work that way.

My recovery doesn't start until I come home, it's going to be a challenge and there are going to be ups and downs. But I'm going to be attending meetings regularly and my life (and your lives) will change for the better. I can't wait for the future. I'm nervous and excited at the same time. The thought of slipping back into my old ways is terrifying. However, all I need to do is work at my recovery and take each day at a time.

Thank you again for always being there.

All my love,

Matt xxx

This letter felt huge to me. It was a real step in the right direction, and a sign that therapy was working. It was also an acknowledgment to myself that there was a long way to go.

***

I loved rehab. It was the first time in my life where I felt like I truly fitted in, and I grew more and more comfortable with myself every single day.

The whole place was a hive of activity from morning until night, and I relished it. We had groups all morning, and in the breaks between groups we would charge to the dining room and eat as many biscuits and as much fruit as we could. Danny was right about my appetite; it came back with a vengeance, and I found I was constantly hungry. The food at mealtimes was good as well; healthy and home-cooked.

Everyone smoked. If I hadn't already been a smoker then I'm sure I would have started; the smoking area was where the best conversation happened, and I never wanted to be left out of that.

Every other evening, we would leave rehab and pile on a minibus to Warrington, where there was a Narcotics Anonymous meeting. I still vividly remember my first meeting as though it was yesterday. I'd been at Oasis for a few days by then, and it was the first time I'd left rehab. I was incredibly nervous; I associated being out sober with enormous anxiety, and I was constantly glancing around. I almost expected someone I knew to appear.

Once the meeting started, I began to settle in, and enjoy myself. All NA meetings run slightly differently, but they all follow the same basic structure: a set of readings, followed by sharing time, and ending with more readings, and the handing out of keyrings to celebrate milestones in clean time. Sometimes there will be a longer reading from the 'Big Book'; the guidebook to how Narcotics Anonymous works, or someone who has significant clean time will talk in length about their recovery. Nowadays, many meetings are held online, or are hybrid, meaning they are available both online and in person. Nevertheless, they still follow that basic structure. My first meeting was no different.

I sat there on that summer evening, listening in awe to the people sharing around me. And when I say in awe, I really mean it. I had never for a second imagined that there were people out there who were like me. I'd honestly believed that my drug problem had been the worst in history, and to hear other people's stories was a relief.

At the end, when the keyrings were handed out, a friend, Alan, tapped me on the knee.

'Go up and get your white keyring, Matt,' he said, 'it's for surrender.'

I did, and the whole room erupted with applause and cheers. Shouts of 'keep coming back' echoed round the hall, and the chair of the group gave me a big hug.

'Well done, mate,' he said. For the first time in a long time, I felt like I actually had done something worth celebrating. I headed back to my seat, unable to stop smiling.

At the next NA meeting, I rustled up enough courage to share.

'Hi,' I said into the silence, 'my name is Matt, and I'm an addict.'

'Hi, Matt,' came a chorus of voices back at me. I felt completely at home.

'This is my first time sharing,' I said, 'so I'm a bit nervous. But I just wanted to say thanks for making me feel so welcome. I do feel really comfortable here, and I relate to so much of what you've all said. My problem with crack got so bad that it nearly broke my family. It wasn't even that long ago, but I look back now, and I feel ashamed of what I did to my mum and dad.'

I told the room some of my horror stories, and some of the times when I'd hurt my mum the most. I told the room how she'd try to stop me going out. I told the room how she'd screamed 'you're ruining my life' after me. I nearly broke down in tears, but when I looked up, the chair of the meeting was nodding as if he completely understood, as were several people sat in the circle. I felt lighter when I'd finished sharing. *This is magical*, I thought. I felt like I'd found my place, and I wanted to grab it with both hands and never let it go.

***

The routine at Oasis was very much the same each day, and I thrived on it. I'd get up early, and take pride in making my bed, shaving, and looking presentable. I was always the first up and about in the morning. I'd make myself a Pot Noodle sandwich for breakfast, chasing it with plenty of water, and several pieces of fruit. When the door to the canteen opened at 8am, I'd dash in there and get my second breakfast. I was always full, and the support workers were amazed by my ability to eat.

After breakfast we'd have a roll-call, just to check that everyone was still there. You were free to just go out in groups for an hour, if none of you were detoxing, and so some people went on little walks. Occasionally people got sick of rehab entirely, and checked themselves out early. To that end, it was important to check who was still there, and who wasn't. After roll-call we began therapeutic duties. These were little cleaning tasks that everyone was assigned; things like re-stocking the toilet roll, or cleaning. In a strange way, I enjoyed doing these. I learned to clean a toilet for the first time in my life, and I took pride in every single little job I was given. I felt like I was looking after myself and my surroundings for once, and I always made sure that I did a good job.

Groups started at 9am, and went on until lunchtime. The afternoons were then filled with other activities, or alternative therapies. We had a gong bath, yoga, and art therapy, and we also headed out for walks when the weather was nice. On Tuesdays, we got the opportunity to go shopping, set free in a shopping centre for a few hours. We relished this time, scampering through the mall like kids on a school trip.

Despite the apparent freedom, we were very much treated like children. Every penny had to be accounted for on shopping trips, and we had to provide receipts for the staff to count it back in. We also weren't allowed mobile phones for the first two weeks, and we were only permitted 10 minutes a day on the landline. I grew to appreciate this time without my phone. Once I was allowed it again in the evenings, I began to see how toxic it was, and how unhealthy the frantic checking of social media could be. Towards the end, I just used my phone for music, using phone time for meditation and reflection, rather than scrolling and liking.

Another strict rule was that we were divided by gender. Men and women were allowed out together, but only if there was more than one of each sex. There also had to be at least three people in total, so if a man and a woman wanted to go out, they had to each find a partner to join them. This never actually affected me, but the one time I left to go swimming there were two women who weren't able to find a third, and therefore weren't able to go.

Not only did the gender rule make outings difficult, but I also found the men much more closed off and unwilling to talk than the women. I wanted to open up, but at times I found that difficult when surrounded by men. At the same time, I can see the sense behind the rule, despite its slightly old-fashioned and heteronormative roots. Rehab can be a difficult time emotionally, and delicate people get attached very easily. Oasis was just doing its best to protect us from that, albeit in a very dated and awkward way.

We entertained ourselves as well during downtime, playing Uno, Chess and Scrabble. We weren't allowed to gamble, so cards were banned, and we ended up making games to keep ourselves occupied. Sometimes entertainment would be as simple as chatting while we smoked, or bursting into an impromptu sing-song.

Evenings were scheduled as well, and we had various activities on the timetable. Sometimes we'd all head out to NA on the minibus, or people went to AA in the local church. Sometimes the support workers would lead half-hearted sessions on various topics. I always hated these.

'Why do I have to come?' I'd whinge, sulking at the back of the room, 'I'd rather be doing step work!'

Sometimes we would have 'peer-led' activities like games and quizzes. I rejected these as well, always keen to get on and do more recovery work. If there's anything I regret about rehab, it's that I didn't get more involved in these activities. Since then, I have learned that recovery is about balance, and this balance comes from all sorts of places. Making new friends and having fun is a key part of this, and I didn't see the importance of this while I was at Oasis.

***

Despite my reluctance to get involved in social activities, I made some really good friends while I was in rehab, many of whom I'm still in touch with today.

My main friend was Darren, a chronic asthma sufferer with a dry sense of humour. Darren and I had an inauspicious start after I made an ill-timed joke during our first group together. He glared at me across the room, and I felt bad immediately. I apologized afterwards, and from then on, we really hit it off. He made huge progress in rehab, and did really well for a while. I think we got on because we were so similar really; we had the same opinions on a lot of issues, and I was happier to speak out than he was. I'd often look at him while I was sharing in group to see him nodding encouragingly along.

I also grew close to Derek, who I looked up to in rehab. He looked after me in his own funny way, making sure I was up in the morning, and always fixing my ever-breaking watch. His military background made him come across as formidable and strict, but he was soft underneath, and really looked out for me. I'd thought at the time that he wasn't going to do well, but I got in touch with him months after rehab and found he was thriving. He has a buzzing social life, and is really happy in his post-alcohol life.

My friend Ricky was also a success, and is someone I continue to keep in touch with. He had a bumpy ride after rehab and relapsed a few times, determined to cling onto his old life. Luckily, he managed to see sense, and is now over a year clean. I regularly visit him in North Wales, and I love watching his journey through sobriety.

Rehab doesn't work for everyone, however, and there were many people who didn't manage to stay clean, with sometimes devastating effects. Shane was a Runcorn local, and was unable to be honest from the start. He said in all the groups that his issue was with crack, but it turned out to be heroin. He relapsed on his first day out of treatment.

Samantha also relapsed. She had a funded place at rehab, and was there for months. This made her unwilling to do any of the work, and she was constantly whinging about wanting to leave. Eventually she did, going back to her mum and dad's house while they were on holiday. She's now fully back into the murky world of crack cocaine.

And then, of course, were the ones who paid the ultimate price for their drug use. William was a young lad in his early twenties, who was constantly in and out of rehab. He maintained the attitude that he was better than his addiction, and that he had it under control. He was held back by his terrifying intelligence; he literally tried to out-think his addiction by learning about every drug he used. He was also complacent about his future; he had plans to relapse as soon as he left, and he knew his grandparents would pay to send him back to rehab if he ever got bad again. Unfortunately, he died just a few months after leaving treatment.

Harriet also died from her addiction very shortly after leaving. She was very quiet in groups, but very talkative outside, and was genuinely excited about her life after treatment. She had a little girl who was three or four, and she constantly talked about her horses and her hobbies. She relapsed almost straight after leaving, and died shortly afterwards.

Darren also died, which at the time was a devastating knock. I still don't know the details of what happened, just that his brother found him dead in his flat in the autumn of that year. The deaths and relapses that came after rehab were all shocking, and I think about every single one of my rehab friends regularly. It's a stark reminder that it can just take one slip to pull you straight back into the world of using, and from there, death is just a short step away. I never let myself forget that.

Chapter 11

Eventually my time in Oasis came to an end. The four weeks flew by, and as my leaving day grew nearer, I felt more and more nervous. By the time the day arrived, I was nearly physically sick with anxiety. I was torn between wanting to start my new life on the outside, and not feeling anywhere near ready. Rehab was a strong safety net for me, and I wasn't sure I was ready to leap without it.

On the day I left, I had a 'graduation' ceremony with all the other residents. Everyone was sat in a circle, with Louise leading the group, and they passed an Oasis keyring around, while each saying a few words about me, and wishing me luck for my future.

'We'll miss you Matt,' they said, 'you've been a clown, but we know you're serious at heart.' The keyring went slowly round that circle, and I felt the love and support coming from every angle. The last of the residents to say goodbye to me was Darren.

'I'll miss you,' he said, 'you always say what I'm thinking.' I looked at him sadly. I knew he struggled to find a voice in Oasis, and I knew that I had been that for him. I was worried about him, and I felt really sad to leave him. The keyring arrived back at Louise, and she smiled encouragingly at me.

'Well, Matt, you say it how it is,' she said, 'I'm squeezing this keyring so it's full of good energy for you,' I remember thinking that was mad. I could barely stop myself from rolling my eyes at the time. I have, however, found myself squeezing it since rehab. I always try to get the good energy out of it when life feels particularly hard. Perhaps there was something in it after all.

I listened to what everyone had to say at graduation, feeling more and more emotional as the keyring went round. I found myself fighting back tears. I had opened up emotionally while at Oasis, but the thought of crying in front of everyone was a barrier I couldn't break through. Instead, I swallowed them down, and gave everyone a brave smile.

'Thanks everyone,' I said, trying not to let my voice crack, 'I'll see you all on the other side.'

Louise stood up, passed me the keyring, and gave me a big hug, while the room erupted in cheers and applause around me. It was a beautiful moment, and a wonderful way to end my time at Oasis. Then it was all over. I was taken to the office and officially checked out. My phone was handed back to me, and I brought my bags down from my room. I was told to wait in the canteen for my taxi, and everyone else headed into group, and that was that.

I stood in that empty room with quiet all around me, suddenly feeling really lost. It was a bizarre feeling; I was weirdly bitter and jealous of everyone up in groups, carrying on without me. In some ways I felt abandoned. I paced up and down, holding my keyring, unsure of what else to do.

'Your taxi's outside, Matt!' shouted the receptionist, and I took a deep breath. I felt like I was about to go on stage in front of thousands of people. Butterflies danced around my stomach, and my heart was beating fast in my chest. This was it. I pressed the door release and stepped, alone, into the fresh air, feeling as though I'd been inside for weeks.

Across the road was a pub, and I looked at it for a moment. *I've got £50 in my pocket...* I thought. And then I snapped out of it, flinging my bags in the open boot, and climbing hastily into the taxi.

'Alright mate,' said the taxi driver, 'how's it been? Good to see someone coming away with a smile on their face!'

'Ah, it was amazing,' I said. It was just a five-minute drive to the train station, but I couldn't shut up. I talked the whole time, telling the driver everything I'd been through. He got my life history from start to finish, crammed at speed into one short journey. I was so proud of being clean, and of how well I'd done.

'Good luck mate,' said the driver as I climbed out, 'I'm proud of you.' It was another lovely moment.

It was a gorgeous August day, hot and sunny, with blue skies stretching for miles. I sat on the platform at Runcorn station beaming from ear to ear. I felt truly amazing; all my nerves about leaving were gone, and I just felt excited to be going home. This was it! This was really it! My new life was waiting for me, and I couldn't wait.

I sat opposite a little old lady on the train, and rang my friend Gavin, keen to share my joy at what I'd achieved.

'Cushty Matty,' he said when he answered, clearly pleased to hear from me, 'what are you doing at this time?''

'Just been released, haven't I?' I joked. The lady opposite glanced quickly at me, looking horrified. I caught her eye, and then looked away again, grinning. I felt like nothing could break through the joy I was feeling.

I emerged from the entrance of Cheltenham Spa station a few hours later, after a change at Birmingham, and immediately had to face one of the pubs I used to drink in frequently. Again, like in Runcorn, I had a moment of weakness. *Just one*, I thought. And then I stopped myself before that could go any further. I walked as fast I could to the taxi rank, and clambered in, giving the driver my mum and dad's address.

It was a really strange drive. Although I'd been joking on the phone to Gavin, I really did feel like I'd been released from prison. The world felt limitless, and yet full of limits at the same time. We went past loads of pubs, and every single one made me feel a bit uneasy. I looked at them all through the windows of the car, knowing that I couldn't go back there for a long time – if ever. I knew I had so much work to do before I'd feel comfortable navigating normal life again.

And then I was home. I walked in the front door, dropping my two bags on the floor, and breathing in the familiar smell of home. My dad heard me come in, and he stepped into the hallway to meet me, beaming from ear to ear. Seeing his face light up filled me with excited joy once more.

'Oh my God, you look so well, son,' he said. He squeezed my arms encouragingly, just as he had when he'd left me in Runcorn. I beamed at him.

'Thanks, Dad,' I said, 'shall we have a cup of tea?'

'Absolutely,' he said, 'after you.'

We took our tea into the living room and just talked and talked. I told him everything, and then repeated it all when Mum came home an hour later. I was so positive and optimistic about life. It felt like a real fresh start for once, rather than one of the fake fresh starts I'd promised myself over and over.

'So, this is really it,' I told them both, 'I mean it this time. This is my fresh start.' They both smiled at me, relief washing through all of us, and I knew that I was on the right path.

I'd been told before I left Oasis that it was really important to get to a meeting straight away, and I'd had every intention to. By the time I was home, however, I just felt knackered, and I really wanted to spend the night with Mum and Dad. We got an Indian takeaway, and settled in for the evening, together. Being home and sober had never felt so good.

***

I knew that I couldn't put off going to NA forever, and so I plucked up the courage to go to a meeting the night after I got home. I was anxious all day, double- and triple-checking the time and location of the meeting on the NA website, and pacing round the house waiting for the evening.

'You okay, Matt?' said Mum several times throughout the day.

'I'm fine,' I snapped back at her. I was really on edge; excited about starting my new life outside of rehab, but also nervous about it. I was worried about seeing people from my old life, and desperate not to return to my old ways.

That night I walked up to the church, my heart beating fast. There was a group of people stood outside, barely visible through a cloud of cigarette smoke. I stood awkwardly on the periphery of the group, trying to make eye contact with someone.

'Hello,' I said, when someone caught my eye, 'is this NA?'

'Hi!' said the man, walking towards me, 'it is! Welcome! I'm Todd.'

I thought he was going to shake my hand, but he enveloped me in a hug, squeezing me to his chest. This is an NA thing, but it made me feel a bit awkward. Todd introduced me to a load of people, and I shook all their hands. I didn't want to hug anyone again. It felt far too weird for me!

Despite the hugging, I had a lovely welcome, and I felt immediately accepted. I had, however, been right to be nervous about seeing people from my old life. I had just walked into the hall, when someone across the room stopped the conversation they were having, and stared at me in disbelief.

'Matty Ingram!' he yelled. I looked more carefully, and saw, to my shock, that it was an old acquaintance from my using days, Curtis, looking me up and down. 'You look so well,' he said, 'I never thought I'd see you in recovery.'

'Alright mate,' I said, pleased in some way to see a familiar face, but struggling to even remember his name through the fog of my memory, 'how's it going?'

Curtis had been from Bishops Cleeve, and had known me as the King of the Sesh from Cheltenham. He still saw my drug usage as inspiring in some ways; he went around that night introducing me to everyone as the big cheese who once did two grams of MCAT in one breath.

'This guy is insane,' he said to everyone, 'never thought he'd quit the drugs. Amazing.'

I nodded and smiled at everyone, feeling an uncomfortable mix of flattered and lost. Curtis's attention had hammered it home to me that drugs had been the entirety of who I was. What was I now without them? I realised that I had to carve out a whole new identity, and that felt very daunting.

I was introduced to a guy called Craig, and I had that strange feeling when you know you know someone, but you don't know how. We nodded at each other, and then made our way to separate sides of the meeting room.

For the next few meetings my paranoia was in overdrive. I knew I'd met Craig somewhere before, but I didn't know if we were friends, or mortal enemies. I could have stolen from him, or fought with him. I just didn't know. Our eyes kept catching during the meetings, and I'd quickly look away nervously.

It finally dropped after a couple of weeks. This was Taz's friend Craig! This was the Craig whose house I'd been in the very first time I met Taz! We were a lot friendlier after that, and I would grin at him every time we were both in a meeting together. I was genuinely glad that he was in recovery – here was another person who'd managed to escape Taz.

That very first meeting out of rehab just felt like a relief. Just the getting there and getting in had felt like a huge amount of effort. I didn't share during that first meeting, but I sat quietly and listened to other people's stories. I felt very grateful to be there.

At the end of the night, they handed out the keyrings celebrating clean time. I finally got to pick up my 30 days. It was a good feeling; very similar to how I felt after doing karaoke in the pub. People were clapping and cheering, and I couldn't stop grinning as I walked back to my seat.

I walked home that night, feeling warm and happy. It was a long walk, but I enjoyed the time to reflect on how far I'd come. I held my orange plastic keyring in my hand like it was my most prized possession.

I started going to that same meeting three times a week. The church was just two minutes' walk from my old flat, and it was strange wandering around the area where I had been so unwell. I would walk past the building my flat had been in and remember how bad things had become. Sometimes I'd even go into the shop where I had bought my whiskey, and pick up a soft drink for the meeting.

Throughout all this, my mum and dad were brilliant. They were endlessly supportive; always happy to take me to a meeting or pick me up if I needed it. They would rearrange anything in their day to make sure I got to NA on time, and were always enthusiastic and interested in my progress.

***

As I began to make friends within the fellowship, I started getting lifts home from meetings with Curtis, and his friend Alistair, who was another NA regular. This is when the first doubts about the fellowship began to creep into my brain.

I'd always thought that NA was built on a solid foundation of respect for other members, and a no-tolerance policy for gossiping. When I was in the car with Curtis and Alistair, I found that – at least in this particular meeting, with these particular people – that wasn't the case. Curtis and Alistair would sit laughing about the other members of the group, taking the piss out of their shares and laying into any display of emotion. I would sit there in silence, uncomfortable with the way people were being talked about, and unsure of where I stood in what was clearly a hierarchy.

I felt that in some ways the bad behaviour displayed by certain members was excused.

'We're all unwell!' someone would cry if someone else behaved badly.

Speak for yourself, I would think, bitterly.

One Saturday morning we went to the Sober Parrot as a group. This is an alcohol-free café in the centre of Cheltenham. It's run by a charity, and provides a safe space for addicts and alcoholics in recovery to socialise.

We'd finished our coffees and were about to pay when Alistair began shuffling past us, and darted out the door, keeping his head down. One by one we paid for ours, and headed outside to join him. It was only when we saw the waitress glaring at him through the window that we realised he hadn't paid, and had absolutely no intention of doing so. It was incredibly embarrassing. Eventually Curtis went back in, and coughed up the cash for Alistair.

'He's unwell,' Curtis said, shrugging, 'he can't help it.' We headed off, but the whole event left a sour taste in my mouth. The Sober Parrot is a wonderful place, and I still go there regularly. To think of someone stealing from them makes me feel really uncomfortable, especially someone who constantly talks about how much of a changed person they are because of the program. The whole thing just felt sly and two-faced. I was also really trying to get away from that 'druggy' stereotype, and being in a group of people who are trying to steal didn't sit well with me. I never went out with Alistair again.

NA itself was beginning to feel a drag as well. The weeks went on, and I began to feel more and more disillusioned with the process, and with the meetings themselves. I wasn't entirely sure why I kept turning up; I was beginning to feel like I wasn't really going anywhere. I heard the same things at every meeting, repeated over and over. I wasn't sure where I was supposed to progress to, or what my next steps should be.

I shared this once in a meeting, and I was advised to get a sponsor. A sponsor is someone who takes you in detail through the Big Book, and helps you work the Twelve Steps. They act as a guide for you, an advisor, and a sounding board for any struggles you face in your sobriety. The advice is always to find someone who you look up to within the programme; someone you really respect. That way you can work towards what they have.

I took this advice on board, and I began looking out for a sponsor. Every meeting I would listen hard and think about whether I would want this person to guide me. The problem was that no-one stuck out. I didn't want the sobriety that anyone else had. In all honesty, I didn't still want to be tied to meetings three times a week in twenty years' time. No-one clicked with me enough for me to ask them, so I kept on the same routine of attending meetings, and keeping a lookout.

One time in a coffee break, I plucked up the courage to say something about how disillusioned I was feeling. I thought that perhaps if I voiced my worries, I'd get some good advice.

'Yeah, you know, I'm not really sure the steps are for me,' I said, feeling nervous even as the words came out of my mouth, 'I'm thinking of trying a different group. SMART maybe?'

There was a collective gasp from everyone in earshot. People were looking at me with wide eyes, as if I had just admitted to some horrendous crime.

'SMART!?' someone said, 'why would you want to do that when the steps are right here?'

'I'm just not sure things are clicking...' I said, my voicing trailing off as I saw the faces of people around me. It was clear that this was not a popular, or much-voiced opinion in NA circles. I wasn't going to get any advice about SMART from these people.

After that, things felt really off for me. In rehab, NA had seemed perfect; like the answer to everything I needed. It had seemed like a place where I really fit in. Now, just for questioning the methods, I felt like I was excluded. Everyone was pleasant to me, but distant, and uninterested, and I began to feel very left out.

The more I questioned why I was there, the fewer answers I seemed to get.

'Have you prayed on it?' people would say in response to me, and I'd feel even more distant from the program.

Sometimes I would be sat in a meeting, and I would really agree with what the sharer was saying. *This is me*, I would think, *this is exactly how I used to feel.* Then their story would go into how they found NA, and I would lose all identification. I didn't relate to finding a Higher Power, or to praying on my problems. I felt shut out of this final stage of the process, and I didn't know how to reach it.

***

It was around Christmas when I reached my limit. Christmas Day for me had always been about getting drunk. The whole day was focused on boozing and then sleeping it off, and without that, I didn't know what to do. I felt like a spare part, and worse, I felt like my bad mood was ruining the day for everyone. By the time evening rolled around I was in such a vile mood I pulled on my coat and headed to an NA meeting in the Catholic Church, unsure of what else to do.

I was still going to three meetings a week like clockwork at this point. I hated them, but I kept coming back, because that's what you were supposed to do. I was terrified of relapse, and of letting my mum and dad down. I didn't feel like the meetings were doing anything, but I had no other tools to keep me sober.

I walked into the church on Christmas evening, and was met with the usual cheerful welcome. My bad mood darkened, however, and I slid into a chair in the circle, unwilling to talk to anyone. Then I realised that Alistair was chairing the meeting, and Curtis was doing the main share. My mood darkened even further when he started to talk. *Ugh*, I thought, *here we go.*

'I want to start this by saying I love you all,' he said, opening his arms and beaming at us all, 'and I couldn't have got to where I am today without the support from every single one of you in this room. You're the best.'

What a two-faced prick, I thought to myself, seething with anger, *he doesn't mean that at all.* As he continued to share, I was flooded with memories of him bitching and whinging in our car journeys on the way home. How could he expect me to trust anything he said?

Just five minutes into his share, I stood up and left. I felt physically sick with anger, and pissed off with NA as a whole. I didn't know how anyone could be so fake, and yet so unanimously believed.

As I stomped home, angrier than ever, I realised that I couldn't let people bug me so much, or it would be a certain road to drinking and using again. But I couldn't see how I could achieve that by remaining within NA. I was stuck and frustrated, and I didn't know what to do.

That Christmas Day meeting was one of the last times I went to NA. I stopped going for good in January 2020, shortly after picking up my six-month keyring. I'd made one final attempt to try and connect with someone, asking an old-timer for advice. Pat had been clean for 17 years, and I thought that if anyone could help me see the NA light, then it would be him.

'Pat,' I said, 'I'm really struggling with NA. I'm just not sure it's for me, and I don't know what to do.' Pat looked at me and smiled blandly.

'Keep coming back,' he said, the generic catchphrase flung out over and over again at every meeting. And with that, my last shred of hope drained from me. How could someone give such useless and generic advice after 17 years, and expect me to want to be like him? I was done. I walked away, my mind made up, and I didn't look back.

I never once regretted leaving NA. The opposite, in fact; I felt liberated and free. I got a few texts in the weeks after asking where I was, and saying that people missed me. I knew they didn't. The texts faded quickly, and I moved on into the next stage of my recovery.

My mum was worried when I told her I wasn't going to meetings anymore. I'd been told that you had to go to meetings or you'd relapse, and I had been regurgitating this to her for months and months now.

'Are you sure this is the right decision, Matt?' she asked me, 'have you called UKAT for advice?'

I had actually phoned a few people about my decision, and received mixed responses. However, several people I liked and trusted had told me that it was important that I find my own path to recovery. I repeated this to my mum, hoping to reassure her.

I was initially unwilling to give up on groups altogether. I attended my first SMART meeting online the night after I left NA. SMART stands for Self-Management and Recovery Training, and it's a course of life skills that helps people stay sober. It also provides another community of like-minded people away from the 12 steps. I had high hopes. I was desperate to find my place in the world again, and I really hoped that SMART would be it.

In some ways the meeting was disheartening. It was very chaotic, and confusing for a newcomer; there was a huge amount of jargon, and it wasn't particularly welcoming. Nevertheless, I liked the concept of it, and it did give me a little flicker of hope. I liked the fact that people only tend to do SMART for a few years; there is an end to the process, and that was something I found refreshing. I also liked the avoidance of labels. Although I am accepting of the fact that I once was addicted to crack, I don't particularly enjoy being labelled as an addict. It's not the end of the world if I am, but I prefer to think of myself as an 'ex-addict', or without a label at all.

Feeling hope again, I bought the SMART Handbook and began working through it in my own time. I thought it was a breath of fresh air, and so useful. I loved the black and white approach to problem-solving; it explained what the problem was, and then it provided a solution. I still go to SMART meetings today, although not particularly regularly.

I am keen to point out that I am absolutely not anti-NA, or anti-12 step fellowships. They absolutely work for some people, and I am so happy for those people who have found sobriety through their programs. The 12 steps provide a really clear and easy-to-follow route into recovery, and their accessibility is next to none. What I do believe, however, is that recovery in other ways is possible, and I consider myself 'pro-choice' as to how this is done. Whether it's Narcotics Anonymous, Alcoholics Anonymous, another 12 Step fellowship, SMART, or something else, if you've found the thing that keeps you sober, then you stick to that. It's your recovery after all.

***

After I stopped NA, I began to make real changes to the way I was living. I'd got lazy while I was attending meetings, thinking that going to NA was all I needed to live life clean and sober. Once I left the fellowship, I realised that I had to take responsibility for my sobriety and my decision-making. This is the point when I believe I really entered into recovery. This changed mind-set coincided with me getting my driving licence back, my drink driving ban over. It felt like another huge step in the right direction.

I had some massive hurdles to overcome. By the start of 2020, my eating had become a real issue. I had begun binge eating while in rehab, and had carried on once I got home. By the time I stopped meetings I was up to around 10 chocolate bars a day. I just didn't feel happy or comfortable unless I was completely full, and I ate almost constantly.

I knew that this was becoming a problem, and I would occasionally make a half-hearted effort to do some exercise, cycling a few slow miles round the local area. When I got home, however, I would reward myself with more food, eating until I was full once more.

On New Year's Eve, I gave up smoking. This was a big positive step for my health in general, but my eating habits worsened for a few months. Every time I got a craving for a cigarette, I would have a Mars bar instead. I was heavier than I had ever been, and I found myself getting out of breath just walking up the stairs to my bedroom. This was a horrible feeling – it reminded me of when I had destroyed my lungs with crack, and I'd struggled to get up the stairs to my flat. The similarities in how I was feeling made me anxious, and I realised I needed to start doing things differently.

This change didn't happen straight away. In the summer of 2020 I was around a year clean and sober. I was happy, stable in my mental health, and positive about how my life was going. I was also significantly overweight, and getting bigger. I had got myself into a routine of being physically lazy; I wasn't working, having chosen to take a gap year after rehab to focus on me. While this was absolutely the right decision for my mental health and my recovery, it meant I wasn't pushing myself physically, and it showed.

By the time the end of my self-imposed gap year came around, I was ready to work again. I sent out my CV, looking for warehouse work, or anything similar to jobs I'd done in the past. I'd been offered an excellent review from my last job before rehab; they'd seen past my problems and realised that underneath it all, I was actually a hard and committed worker. I didn't need the reference in the end, but the show of support gave me the confidence spurt I needed to begin making applications.

One of the jobs I applied for was in the Asda warehouse in Bristol, and I was invited to interview. When I arrived, I immediately got a good feeling. It felt like the right place to be, and the right time to start work. I went with my gut, and accepted the job, starting almost immediately.

That was when I hit a hurdle. It was very physical work; there was lots of lifting and carrying, and initially I found myself completely unable to do it. I spent the entire day sweating and out of breath, working at a much slower pace than my colleagues. A day at work was too much for me physically, and I would come home exhausted and depressed, feeling like I was a failure.

I then realised that this was the kick in the arse I needed to really make that lifestyle change I'd been talking about for so long. I stuck at the job, persevering even when it was tough, and I took control of my eating habits, cutting out the chocolate, and choosing healthier snacks instead. Slowly, my weight began to creep down, and I felt myself getting fitter.

In March of 2021 I made another big step towards my fitness, and started the Couch to 5K program. I had never been a runner, but I wanted another goal, and another way to push myself, and I began following the program regularly.

I won't lie - I hated it for a long time. My early morning runs filled me with dread, and as winter drew in, it took all my strength to climb out of bed and drag myself out of the front door. Slowly, though, I began to enjoy my running. My increased distances began to fill me with a real sense of joy and achievement, and as the summer rolled round, I found myself looking forward to my runs, and the relaxed warmth I felt after them. Running is now a huge part of my life, and I am so glad I made that leap.

***

Recovery has not just been smiles and successes. In June of 2020, I faced the biggest test of my recovery that I've had to date. It was a real shock, and the fact that I managed to get through it showed me how far I had come since rehab.

I was driving to my Gran's house one breezy summer's day, when I saw Dale, Deb's boyfriend. I stuck my thumb out the window and waved at him, but I didn't stop. We were all on speaking terms again, but it had never been quite the same after the falling out. As I accelerated away, I noticed him in my rear-view mirror, frantically waving his arms in an attempt to get me to stop. Concerned, I pulled over, and I wound my window down as he jogged towards the car.

'What's up?' I said, and he looked at me sadly.

'It's Debbie,' he said, 'she's in hospital.' This didn't worry me. Not initially. Deb had always suffered with her physical health (almost certainly as a result of her heavy drinking), and she had been in and out of hospital a lot over the years. She always bounced back.

'She'll pull through,' I said. Dale shook his head.

'No, it's really serious, Matt,' he replied, 'she's only got a 10% chance of waking up.' His eyes welled up as he spoke, and he wiped furiously at his cheek with the heel of his hand. I just stared at him, confused. I'd driven past Deb's flat just a week ago, and she had been full of laughter, sunning herself out in the front garden with a gang of friends.

'Hang on,' I said to Dale, 'what do you mean 'wake up'? Is she asleep? What's going on?' Dale just looked at me, still swallowing back tears. I listened to what I had just said, the words hanging in the air, and I realised that Deb was in a coma. This was far more serious than anything she'd ever been through before.

'Yeah…' said Dale. He didn't quite know what to say, and neither did I.

'Well,' I said, swallowing hard, 'let me know if there's anything I can do to help?' I drove off in a bit of a panic, mumbling excuses about having to get to my Gran's. And then, as I was driving, it hit me. Deb was going to die, and I needed to say goodbye. I dialled Dale from the hands-free device in my car.

'Please Dale,' I said, stumbling over my words, 'I know we fell out, but I need to say goodbye. I'm sorry, I need to say goodbye. She was like a big sister to me!'

'I'll do my best, Matt,' he said, fighting back tears. This was in the very middle of the COVID-19 pandemic, and the UK was only just beginning to creep out of the first full lockdown. Hospital visits were seriously limited, but I was determined to get in there to see her. I just kept driving, unsure of what else to do, suddenly dying for a drink to chase the pain away.

Luckily, I had enough tools under my belt by then to know that this was not an option for me. Gritting my teeth, I drove home, and then called my mum, telling her everything that had happened. I paced up and down, still desperate for a drink, but determined not to have one. I succeeded.

The next day I received a phone call from Dale.

'Hi Matt,' he said, and I could tell from his voice that it was bad news. 'You can't visit, I'm afraid. It's family only, and her condition has worsened; she can't have any visitors at all at the moment.'

'Okay,' I said, my eyes swimming with tears once again, 'can you tell her that Bambi loves her more than anything, and goodbye?' Bambi had been her pet name for me; she'd called it me on the first day she met me, when I could hardly stand up after drinking too much vodka.

'Like Bambi on ice, you are!' she'd laughed, and the nickname had stuck.

Dale rang me back the next day.

'I told her Bambi loves her, and I know she heard it,' he told me. 'She squeezed my hand when I said it, and her eyes flickered a little bit.'

'Thanks Dale,' I said, hanging up the phone. I burst into tears straight away, both from grief and from relief that she'd got my message. Knowing that I'd got through to her was the closure I needed. I was very sad that I wasn't going to get to see her, or be there as she died, but I was relieved that I'd been in her thoughts right at the end. She held on for another day or two, but passed away peacefully not long after that phone call.

The grieving period was complicated for me. I did feel very sad, but in an empty sort of way. I was also able to appreciate the space I'd had from her for a few years. I knew that she would have looked after me in my darkest times, and quite possibly I'd have never even tried crack if we'd stayed close. However, I knew that if I'd had to face her death without a good stable recovery behind me, I would have relapsed. In that way, it was a blessing that we hadn't been quite as close at the end.

The funeral was a few weeks later, and, because of the pandemic, numbers were limited. I was determined this time, however, to make sure I didn't miss out, and both Dale and Deb's mum were supportive of me attending.

'You'll batter the doors down to get in anyway, won't you?' said Deb's mum. She had a point.

Deb was loved, and her funeral made this clear. Despite the numbers being limited, there were around 20 or 30 people waiting outside. They knew that they wouldn't be able to get in, but they wanted to be there to pay their respects. And, as it turned out, in the end, they could all attend. Restrictions on funerals had been lifted that morning. It felt like a sign; Deb deserved to be celebrated.

The funeral itself was awful, as all funerals are. I began to cry the moment I saw the car carrying her coffin rounding the corner, and I struggled to stop for the entire day. I was weeping quietly throughout the service, unashamed in my grief. The celebrant read out Deb's life history to begin, and I was slightly gutted that I was missed out of it completely. I knew, though, that I had been a huge part of her life, acknowledged in the funeral or not.

At the end of the service, Sweet Caroline was played. This had been our song – she had loved it, and I would always sing it to her at the end of a messy night. She always said that I nailed it. I grinned through my tears as the coffin passed through the curtains, and then it was over, and we shuffled tearily outside.

'You coming to our house for a drink, Matt?' asked Deb's brother Harry, and I shook my head. I was strong in my recovery, but not strong enough for that. I said my goodbyes and headed home, taking the evening to reflect on the beautiful friendship that Deb and I had.

In some ways, I hugely regretted falling out with Deb. I knew that if we'd stayed close friends then life would have been very different, and for a while I let myself think that I'd have been happier. But then I thought more deeply into my past. I realised that I would almost certainly have ended up on the path to addiction eventually, and falling out with Deb only made it happen sooner. In that way, therefore, I was grateful for what had happened between us. I still think about her every day. She was a huge part of my life, and she shaped my future. I was lucky to have known her.

***

In November 2020, just a few months after Deb's death, I got a call from Douglas, another friend from rehab. We'd kept in touch with one another, and regularly interacted on the UKAT Alumni Facebook page, which was a group for anyone who'd been through a UKAT facility. I'd taken to sharing on there in recent months, and had made a bit of a name for myself for being 'anti-NA' (which, of course, isn't true). Nevertheless, my opinions on being able to find your own path to recovery were often unwelcome, and I had got into a fair number of online arguments.

When Douglas called me, I was happy to hear from him, as I always was with any of my rehab friends.

'Doug!' I said, 'what's up?' We chatted for a few minutes, just catching up about what had been going on in each other's lives, and then we got on to talking about the future.

'I have an idea, Matt, and I wanted to suggest something to you,' Doug said. I was immediately intrigued.

'What?'

'Well, you've always had really good and strong ideas, and I think you've got a way with words as well. I think you should start a blog,' he said. I paused.

'What's a blog?' I asked, laughing. He explained everything to me, how it would be a platform for me to share my ideas and my journey with the world. That way I could spread my message, and also avoid arguments on the UKAT page. I left the conversation feeling thoughtful, with a little bud of excitement deep inside me.

Endless Possibilities didn't spring up straight away, but it didn't take long. I began researching blogging that night, and seriously considered what it would take. I began brainstorming names, and talking to people close to me about the idea. Just a few days later I went live on Facebook, sharing it on my personal Facebook page, and on the UKAT Alumni page. I then joined every Facebook bulletin board I could, from up and down the country, and promoted it on there, advertising it as a new space to follow my journey and find your own way into recovery.

Slowly but surely, the page began to take off. With every new post, I gained more followers, and people began to say that I was an inspiration. They thanked me for sharing, saying I was providing a fresh new voice to recovery circles. Before long I was getting 200 to 300 new followers with every post, and reached 20,000 followers within a matter of months. Since then, it's just been organic growth. It's exploded, and it continues to grow.

Endless Possibilities helps me stay sober in so many ways. It's an outlet for me; I find it so helpful to get my thoughts and feelings down on paper, and receive feedback on what I'm going through. The page has also created a really tight-knit support network, and I know there are many people who would be there for me if I was struggling. Of course, the page helps others as well, which helps me in turn. I get a real buzz from knowing that my words are out there changing lives. It's an amazing feeling, and it can't be replicated. I love what I have created, and I have never been prouder of anything in my life.

Chapter 12

That's the story of how I got to where I am today, and how Endless Possibilities was born. But it is in no way the end of my recovery journey. There is so much more I want to do, and there is so much more that I *need* to do. If I have learned anything through my time in recovery, it's that staying clean and sober takes constant work. Taking a day off my recovery is not an option – I will be working at it for the rest of my life.

My path hasn't followed a 12-step program, but, once again, I would like to reinforce that I am not anti-12 steps. In some ways I am envious of those who have found sobriety through the fellowships; it's a route to sobriety that is much more accessible than building your own path, and it comes with its own ready-made community.

I do take some bits from the 12 steps. One of them is the concept of God or a Higher Power. This is something I really struggled with in rehab, and hugely over-complicated. At its core, 'God' just means a power greater than yourself – it's not about religion at all. For me, my Higher Power is that little voice inside you that tells you when you're doing something wrong. Call it karma, or call it conscience, I like to imagine it as a little man sat on my shoulder telling me the right thing to do. There is still that man on my other shoulder, trying to tempt me down a bad road. These days I do everything I can to listen to the voice that knows what's right.

The word God absolutely shouldn't put anyone off taking the 12-step route into recovery. In fact, I don't really think the word should be used at all; it's really difficult to display the 12 steps as non-religious when the word 'God' is front and centre in all the literature and posters. Really, it's not about God. It's about finding something outside of yourself to guide you. Find what works for you.

I think the fellowships need expanding and modernizing. I believe that they need a shake-up, and they need to rid themselves of some of the stranger traditions that now seem outdated and old-fashioned. Things like the chanting and holding hands at the end, and the strict rules on relationships between different genders. These things can seem weird and scary to the newcomer, and I think that they put a lot of people off. I also recognize that this is none of my business. They work for millions of people worldwide, and who am I to criticize that?

Not working the 12 steps doesn't mean I don't have to work hard on myself, or that my path is somehow easier. In fact, I put effort into my recovery every single moment that I am awake. I never let myself forget how easy it would be to slip down back into that world of drink and drugs, and that is somewhere I never want to go back to.

The foundation of my recovery is being a good person, and I work at this constantly; doing the right thing is how I get my warmth these days. I think that helping others is one of the biggest things that keeps me clean, and I truly believe that anyone who is serious about maintaining sustainable recovery needs to help other people in some way. I aim to do this daily through my writing and sharing on Endless Possibilities, and being open and honest about my struggles in recovery to my followers. It warms my heart when someone reaches out to me and tells me that I have made a difference to their life, and I hope I can continue making a difference for a long time.

Being a good person and making good decisions isn't just about making big outward gestures like Endless Possibilities, or contributing to a support network. It also means making the right decisions on little things that affect only me. For example, I regularly eat apples nowadays. I don't like apples – I think they're boring. In my using days, I would have genuinely considered an apple too dull to even consider eating. I survived on fun and fast foods, like chocolate, crisps and general junk, and that's if I ate at all. But now I know that life gets better and better when you work a little harder for it. I have entirely changed my attitude to myself, and the way I see the world. I make sure all the little things are in place: eating healthily, drinking plenty of water, and exercising frequently. I get plenty of sleep, I go to the dentist regularly, and I watch my caffeine intake. These all sound like little things, but they're really important to help me feel good about myself, and to keep my sobriety on track.

I also recognize the need to keep myself in check, and to not let my ego run away with me. I am certain that losing sight of reality would put me straight on the road to relapse, and I know that I need to avoid that. Early on in my Endless Possibilities days, I posted something about how pleased I was with my blog, and how I hoped it was helping others. The outpouring of validation was huge, but within that I received a comment that really made me stop and think. *Just be careful when it all quietens down*, it said, and I think about this a lot. I need to remain wary that things might get a bit slower, or even stop altogether, and I need to be prepared for this. If Endless Possibilities were to shut down for some reason, I need enough tools behind me that I wouldn't immediately turn to drink and drugs. This is why it's so important for me to be a good person outside of the blog as well. Endless Possibilities cannot be my entire life – that would be far too dangerous.

I often have to take a step back and analyse how things are going in my life. Things are moving very fast; Endless Possibilities is exploding, and more and more doors are opening for me every single day. I have to be careful not to get overly swept up or stressed about these things. It's really important for me to set aside time to reflect, and to take some healthy mental space. I do this with meditation, regular practice of mindfulness, and plenty of self-care. Much of this is achieved through exercise, believe it or not. The change in me is just enormous!

***

And, of course, at just over two years clean, the story is only just beginning. I have so many hopes and dreams for my future now that drugs are out of the picture, and I'm so excited to get going on all of them. In the short term, I would like to see Endless Possibilities grow. I want to take it full time eventually, so I can leave my job in the warehouse. I don't just want this for my own sake; I want my blog to reach as many people as I can. Although it started just as my story, it has developed into a support group in its own right, and I would love that to expand. Ideally, I hope to see it double in growth, if not more. I always look at why I started the blog, the taglines I have all over my Facebook page: Raising Awareness, Breaking Stigmas and Helping People. If I can do more of that, then I will be happy.

Away from the blog, I would like to go back into education, studying Counselling, or another subject that will allow me to help others. I also want running to remain a huge part of my life. Unbelievably, I am now training for a half-marathon, and I hope that there is a marathon in my future somewhere. Whatever happens, I hope my fitness continues to improve.

In the long-term, I would love to open up my own residential rehab facility. I always imagine this as being on the Isle of Wight, as this is one of my absolute favourite places. In reality, it could be anywhere, I just want to make it happen. My rehab, when it opens, will be family- or support network-orientated. I have always thought that rehabs should be more focused on the entire family unit, and on the life outside of rehab walls.

I'd also like my rehab to have a better aftercare program. At Oasis, I was invited back once a week for a process group with a counsellor. While I always found this time really helpful, I never thought this was enough. For those who don't have the same level of support that I did, one weekly group therapy session is insufficient. I would like to build a really strong community spirit for those who go through my rehab, and make sure everyone feels very supported afterwards.

I have personal long-term goals as well. I'd love to get married and have children one day, and I want to eventually buy my own house. If I keep on track, I have no doubt that I will achieve these goals in good time.

Even though life is really just beginning, I can see how wonderful things have become for me already. My relationship with my parents has never been better. Of course, we still have arguments, but these are normal arguments about washing up or leaving clothes on the bathroom floor. It's not perfect, but it is 100 times better for all of us than being in active addiction. I actually very much enjoy my parents' company these days. I feel very grateful for the vast amount of support they have always given me, and continue to give. That being said, I am looking forward to eventually moving out and getting my own place. But that's in the future – for now, I am just making up for lost time with them.

My relationships with my friends have also improved. There was a lot of talk in rehab about cutting toxic people out of your life, but I didn't do that. I didn't have to. I realised that when I changed enough, the friends who were only using me for drugs just drifted away naturally. On the flip side, the friends who I pushed away in active addiction have come back into my life, and that is an incredible blessing. Now, instead of being the erratic and worryingly loud friend who was constantly on drugs, I am full of energy and always up for something exciting. Sure, we can't drink together anymore, but instead we go on long walks and road trips, or we have meals out. I also gained a huge brand-new support network of people in recovery, mainly people from rehab who I have kept in touch with. I definitely lost some people in recovery, but the ones I gained back made it worth it.

Life has become better in so many little ways. Now I'm not spending every penny I have on drink and drugs, I am able to save, and treat myself when I would like something. I took a little solo trip to the Isle of Wight recently, something I would never have been able to do (or wanted to do) in active addiction. I now appreciate my days off work as time to rest and refocus, rather than using them to get as drunk or high as I possibly can. I take pleasure in the smallest things, like getting an early night, or having a really good cup of tea. My hard work is paying off at work as well; I was recently nominated for Employee of the Month, out of 400 people who work at the warehouse. It feels so amazing to go into work every day with a smile on my face, not making excuses for why I'm late or stinking of booze.

That little creeping feeling of anxiety that I've felt throughout my life never fully disappeared, and maybe it never will, but it is so much smaller now I am not feeding it with substances. I also finally addressed the PTSD from my accident with counselling, and I released all my years of pent-up emotion. That was a huge relief, and since attending therapy, I have found my PTSD hasn't bothered me anywhere near as much. I wake up each morning happy to be alive, and grateful for the life I have created for myself. I am lucky, and I am grateful for what I have been given.

To finish, let me summarize my thoughts and feelings on my recovery. In short, let me tell you what I believe to be true.

At some point, when your drinking and using reaches a certain point, you step through a door, and you slam it shut behind you. You have left the World of Normal Using, and you have entered Addiction. Once you have come through this door, there is no going back. It's a one-way door only. Sorry about that.

Ahead of you, you then have a choice. One door is the Using Door. You can go through that one if you choose. It will be easier to take that door, that's for sure. It might even be fun at first. But the further you go down the Using Hallway, the less fun it gets. It also gets harder to turn back. At the end of the Using Hallway there is a door with one word on it; Death. Many, many addicts choose the Using Door, and barrel down it to Death, without ever looking back. Death, is of course, a one-way door also.

Happily, you have another option. You can choose to take the Recovery Door. This will be hard work, and it will take considerable effort to get it open. You might even give up a few times, and go back through the Using Door. You'll find, however, that each time it gets harder to come back through. You'll hurt more people, and you'll lose more of yourself each time. But, if you can get through the Recovery Door, you will find that it is the exact opposite to the Using Door. It is hard at first, but it gets easier and easier the further down that hallway you go. You can, of course, turn back, and go back to the Using Door, but the further down you get, the less you want to. Death is at the end of Recovery as well, of course. Ultimately there is no getting away from Death. But Death in Recovery is much harder to see. It isn't there, constantly in view. It's hidden, round twists and turns of corridors that are filled with reward after reward.

Why is it so hard? Why can't everyone make it into the Recovery Hallway? The answer to this is simple. Because in order to stay there, you have to change the way you think completely. Getting good, solid recovery means changing what you value. It means owning everything you did wrong, and apologising for it. It means quickly identifying when you make mistakes, and apologising for them too. It means helping others for no other reason than to help them. In short, it means doing your absolute best to always do the right thing.

As I've said many times, I don't think a 12-step program is the only way to get better. I say that with a warning, however. What is, undeniably, needed to get better is the complete change of attitude and values described above. This is non-negotiable. The 12 Steps will get you there, and they will get you there simply, with everything set out in front of you. If you choose not to go down a 12 Step route, then you need to find yourself another way to get to that altered mind-set.

My recovery, and therefore my altered way of thinking, is based on a program of my own making. I take bits from everywhere, building a guide to living that works for me. Essentially, it involves making a conscious effort to do the Next Right Thing. That's the Right Thing for others, not just myself. I take pride in being reliable, thoughtful and helpful. I am polite and cheerful whenever possible. I am never late for work, I never pull a sickie, and I never slack off just because it would be easier. I apologised to my parents, and I continue to apologise whenever I do something wrong. Whenever there is conflict in my life, I look at whether I had a part to play, and if I did, I do my best to right the wrong.

I no longer go to Narcotics Anonymous, or Alcoholics Anonymous, or any fellowship meetings. But I still have a great respect for their program, the steps, and the way they have guided so many people into recovery. It's incredible that we have that free resource on our doorstep, and when people come to me asking for help, that's where I always direct them at first. When I go to a meeting, it is always a SMART meeting, and I would advise this for anyone who is struggling to make the steps click.

Constantly trying to be a better person is hard work, and sometimes I fail. Sometimes I do the wrong thing; I leave my washing up in the sink, or I say something snappy to one of my parents. But that's okay too, because I always apologise when I see where I have gone wrong. As long as I don't stop trying to be a good person, as long as I don't stop learning and growing, all will be well. And already all my hard work has rewarded me with a life beyond what I could have ever expected.

There is a passage in the AA Big Book called The Promises. It's read out at most meetings, especially when there are newcomers in the room, because it describes to you exactly what you can get if you choose recovery. Very simply, it makes several promises of what can be expected if you work hard for your recovery, acknowledging your faults, helping others, and trying to grow as a human. It promises that if you work really hard at your recovery, you'll be amazed at the results. It promises that you will know freedom, and peace, and joy. It promises that your messy past will help you shape your future, and you'll see how you can use your own experiences to benefit others. It promises that you won't regret anything you've been through. It promises that you'll think far less about yourself, and far more about others. It promises that you will understand how to handle life. Above all, it promises that everything about your life will change for the better.

I, without doubt, have found all of this to be true.

Acknowledgements

Mum and Dad

The biggest thanks has to go to my parents. Without your love and support I honestly don't know where I'd be right now. You deserve the world and so much more for the amount of stuff you've had to put up with. I love you both very much.

John Paul

Thank you to my cousin who I've looked up to since I was a kid. You've always had my back, through the good times and the bad, and I shall be forever grateful. I got there in the end, Cuz!

Uncle Rog

Thank you to my Uncle Rog for all of the support, encouragement and lovely food you cook for me when I visit. Nothing beats coming to see you and getting away from Cheltenham for a few hours and I'm extremely grateful to have you in my life.

Gran

Thank you to my Gran for providing me with a sanctuary when I was struggling for all those years. A place where I could go, no questions asked, and eat you out of house and home. A place full of love that I still visit all the time today. You might moan at me non-stop but I know it's because you love me - I love you too.

Nan

Thank you Nan, my guardian angel. You may have passed away when I was just 10, but you are still one of the most inspirational people I have ever met. I think the fact you made a record of your life planted the seed in me to write this book. In a way, I'm glad you only knew me as a sweet and innocent little boy with his whole life ahead of him, but I really hope you'd be proud of me now. Lots of love, Matthew.

The rest of my family

Thank you to all of my family members from both sides who have helped me, supported me, encouraged me and, most importantly, been there for me. I may not have seen much of you in person over the years, mostly out of shame and embarrassment, but I hope I've made you proud and I can't thank you enough for all of the kind messages I've had since getting myself sorted. I love you all.

Elizabeth Burton-Phillips MBE

Thank you for your support and guidance and all of the wonderful work you and everyone else does at DrugFAM, you are all absolutely amazing.

Francesca

Thank you so much for helping me with, not only the website and the book, but for making me believe in myself and giving me the confidence to push myself that little bit further in life. I'm not sure where I'd be without you and all of our meetings!

Hebe

Thank you to Hebe for ghostwriting this and managing to put my waffle into a book that makes sense - that must have taken some doing!

Kirsty, Fay and family

Thank you for putting up with my nonsense for so many years and always being there when I've needed you. From allowing me to stay on your sofas to keeping me company while I've been struggling. You've all played a massive part in my life and you continue to do so. There's way too many of you to name but I love you all!

Simon and Jimbo

Thank you both for being there through the worst times and now the best times. You are friends that are more like family and no matter how long we don't speak, we always pick up where we left off which shows how special our bonds are.

The rest of my friends

Alex, Mark, Scotty and to all of you I've missed and the ones I don't see much anymore, you still hold a special place in my heart and always will. Lisa and everyone at the pub and all of my friends around Cheltenham - thank you for the good times and I hope I'm making you proud with my new life. I love you all and miss you very much.

The Kerton's

You deserve a special mention for being like my extended family from the other side of the country. It's such a shame we live so far away but our friendship is one of the best things to come out of my recovery journey. See you soon, love you all.

The Rehab Lot

I can't name you all because there's just so many of you, but special shoutout to Little Stevie, Becky, David, Trev, Peter, Linda, Lisa, Sophie, Dan, Andy and anyone else I attended Oasis Runcorn with, including all of the staff of course. You've played a massive part in my journey and I'm so grateful to have made friends for life with lots of you. And not forgetting those who I've not named because you'd probably wish to remain anonymous (you know who you are) I wish you the very best for the future. I love you all, look after yourselves.

The Endless Possibilities Community

I wouldn't be where I am today without the love, support and encouragement of everyone who follows Endless Possibilities on social media. Thank you all so much, from the bottom of my heart, for letting me share my life with you and helping me stay in recovery.

Printed in Great Britain
by Amazon

78305572R10098